AF239916

Messages of Peace
from
the Pleiades

Helena Öhrström

© 2014 Helena Öhrström

Print: Books on Demand GmbH, Norderstedt, Germany
ISBN: 978-91-7463-476-1
Cover image: Sissela Winberg
Translator: Marianne Jensen-Rose

info@avalonskolan.se
www.avalonskolan.se
www.essences.se

Thank you and thoughts of gratitude to all wonderful people, family as well as students, friends and teachers throughout my spiritual development. Along with the habitants of the Pleiades they have been and still are of support, encouragement and as sources of inspiration.

They have with great patience been helpful in the process, making it possible for this book to be written.

I would also like to pay thanks to Inger Dimblad for the help with spelling and grammars. Lotte Mjöberg for sharing fantastic advices in how to design a book. She has been supportive and given positive feedback in a constructive way.

I would like to thank my beloved children who are constant sources of inspiration to me and for having faith in me.

Finally my dearest husband who had faith in me and encouraged me in every possible way. He has patiently helped me with continuing the completion of the Peace messages from the Pleaides.

With love peace and light

Helena Öhrström

Introduction

My name is Helena and since many years now I work as a Medium contacting the spirit world. I´m also teaching energy medicine and healing as well as being a channel for producing Inner Peace essences. Being in contact with the spirit world is everyday life to me and at times you could say I'm just as much there as here.

It´s a fun and inspiring work and I feel profound joy and pleasure helping people and animal in this way. In the autumn of 2009 this everyday life changed into, me one day being able to hear messages. What came as messages was meant to be communicated out into the world to other people. I was told these messages came telepathically and they were messages from the Pleiades.

When the first message came I thought I was imagining, but after persistent persuasion from their side, I finally gave up. You know how it´s like when a song gets stuck inside your head and it never stops. It was exactly like that, but instead of a song, there was the messages from them repeating themselves.

After I had written the first message, nearly a year of silence followed. I had almost forgotten about it when it hit at full force in my mind and urged me to write again.

At the time I was rather tired and lacking of energy, so when the habitants from the Pleiades woke me up in the middle of the night I didn´t welcome the messages with joy. I was probably pretty sulky about not getting my sleep. But quite quickly I realized I just had to put up with it or as they say like the situation and make the best of being awakened at two-three o´clock in the night to write.

Most of the time I was half a sleep and as I afterwards realize much easier to get in contact with in that state.

I have learned from the habitants of the Pleiades, when we read the telepathic texts from the habitants of the Pleiades, it affects our cellular memory and DNA and we receive a part of their energy. We don´t have to understand everything or believe in it to be affected in a positive way. The text and the words which are transferred telepathically can sometimes sound pompous. Words like beloved children and collaborator are their choice of words and way of seeing things from their dimension.

Don´t put any valuations into this, but look upon it as a game and an experiment involving yourself just to be open minded and see what happens. The habitants of the Pleiades believe the text being transferred telepathically are vibrations of light, love and peace. This can be absorbed by your light body to help heal all of the old pain and events affecting your life in a negative way.

If you like, you can read it as if they speak directly to you. There is a healing energy in everything and you use the book at your own wish. It´s also knowing us living in a time of changes with ourselves and our Earth, the words of the inhabitants of the Pleiades can be helpful to us and to create more peace on our planet.
So, I hereby invite you to this fantastic adventure of meeting the habitants of the Pleiades and their energy, which is full of love and healing vibrations. The habitants of the Pleiades would like to help us find more happiness, harmony and peace with ourselves and our Earth.
But first some information about the Plciades.
Have a nice journey!

About the Pleiades

The Pleiades is an open cluster of stars in the constellation of Taurus the Bull and achieved its name after the Greek mythology's name of the seven nymphs, daughters of Atlas and Pleione. The star cluster is also known as the Sevenstars or the Seven Sisters.

The Pleiades are situated about 380 light years from the Sun. With the naked eye, the Pleiades look like a tiny Big Dipper and one can typically see six of the brightest stars included in the star cluster, but under good visibility conditions you can see up to ten. In a pair of ordinary binoculars a variety of additional stars reveals themselves and in total it includes some hundred.

The stars are surrounded by a nebula, which can be seen in photographs where a long exposure time has been used. The star cluster is relatively young, about 100 million years, and is believed to stay merged for another 250 million years ahead.

Here follows a description from the habitants of the Pleiades about themselves.

Now we wish to tell you about ourselves, to help you imagine us and understand our friendship and love for you human children and collaborators on earth. We consist of energy, a more ethereal form of energy than your structural form of energy. Our energy can change shape and colour and the frequency is in higher tones than the ones you have on earth.

Our so called bodies are more transparent and we do not age in the same way as you earthlings do. We fill up energy with light and do not feed the same way you do.
We live in groups of harmonious souls. Love, peace and light is the foundation for our being and life. Joy, happiness and harmony is our daily song.
We speak telepathically to each other and have the ability to converge and merge with each other. In this way we form a unity allowing us to absorb one and others energy and new vibrations and tones occur.
The animals and the children "belong" to all of us and through community and love we nourish and bring wisdom to their development. We converge in big groups, where we exchange love energies, joy, humour and where we can meditate and make telepathic journeys throughout the universe.
Plants and nature do not look like the ones you have on earth, we live in different colours and vibrations empowering us.

Through the colours and vibrations we experience and are part of a so called nature and it all coalesce. Water is present in the shape of steam, it is a natural part of us.

We are the opposites of you, i.e. what you dream about in your dreams and the same energy where you find your selves at that time.

9

You are the matter we are the non-matter. In times like these we are getting closer to each other, our energies are getting closer to each other.

Light meets darkness, happiness meets sorrow, anger and control. These are certainly monumental times. Dear human children we are aware of your work and that it feels difficult and heavy.

Have faith and trust.

Times of joy, love, peace and light awaits you.

Message of Peace from the Pleiades

*Dear, dear collaborators we have awaited you for a long time.
We have been holding our light above you, whispering in your
ear, rocked you to sleep and spoken to you in your dreams. We
are so grateful you have now accepted a cooperation with us
habitants of the Pleiades. We send Love, light and peace.*

*You have been chosen for a reason. The reason is you are one of
us, but you are also a mediator from us to you.
It has been a long time now, millions of years.
Dear children finally you have come home
We blow a fanfare to the universe that the message is received.*

*We will now in the pace you wish for transfer telepathic
information for you to communicate to thousands and thousands
of people.
We bring you the key to the universe and you open it as you
please.
You are a child of Peace and with the message of peace you will
now go out into the world.
Your own story of the peace will be written and read by others.
We cannot well enough express our thankfulness for your
cooperation with us.*

*What do you wish for?
Speak your wish and so will be it.
Know in your heart that is the truth.
When you are touched by your feelings you will know the
answer.
The feeling is the answer to your questions.*

You believe you have to think, but the feeling is the objective of thoughts.
The thought is the workspace and the feeling is the product made at the workspace.
You seek for answers, outside your selves. To seek answers outside your selves is like asking somebody else what your favourite food or colour is.
You carry all the answers within you.
You have been taught from darkness the answers will be found from somewhere else and not from your selves.
Light tells you, you know everything within your selves.

You carry so much within which is meant to be exposed, a channel of light and vibrating colours.
What fantastic colours you are.
Layers of darkness have been peeled off and you are very beautiful.
The work you have done have occasionally been hurtful and with pain. Many tears have fallen down your cheek. You have felt week, small, insignificant and tattered.
Look now and luck has turned and you will appear as a newly cut diamond from a grindstone.
It glistens and shimmers, it is so beautiful.
Put up boundaries when others want to steal your shimmer, ask them to find their own inner self.

So time went by, nearly a whole year of silence and I had almost forgotten about the contact with the Pleiades. Until one night in the winter of 2010 I was once again wakened in the midst of my sleep. I could sense these fantastic light beings around my bed and the notion if I was sleeping or awake was difficult to decide.

I couldn't go back to sleep, but heard in my mind it was time again to receive telepathic messages. So I dragged myself to the kitchen table, took out a notebook and a pen and let the hand move like in a dream to see the sentences and words emerging. This winter was brighter than usual and already in late November the snow was like a warm and soft duvet, covering the surroundings of our farm in the southern countryside. The snow stayed for a long time, yes almost three months, which is very uncommon here in the province of Skane.

An intense period of work during the night took off and after falling asleep in the couch early in the evening I was sleepwalking to my bed just to be awakened between two and four o´clock in the night.

At the beginning I pretended as if nothing happened and tried to get back to sleep again. I felt a certain resistance towards the nightly work. But it turned out to be futile and I had to get up anyway in the end.

In the morning my husband and kids find me sitting by the kitchen table with my hair on end, in my morning gown and slippers and at this point, I as well as all these things were quite worn out.

Oh well these are worldly things and as you will probably have understood by now, I'm just an ordinary person with, what some people may say, a few unusual abilities.

So following is the continuation of the telepathic messages from the Pleiades.

These messages are a mixture of a story from my life and the messages from the Pleiades and in the way they asked for and guided me to write. All of this creates a web of words, colours and vibrations. It's a part of the web of my life entwined with fantastic messages of peace from the Pleiades and I would like to share this web with you. It's apparently a part of the life tasks I took on the day I descended to earth this time. It's nothing I remember, but learned on the way steadily leading me forward.

In retrospective one can see a red thread of happenings and meetings with different people. What a fantastic thought, us having directed and chosen, but also adopted various life challenges for our spiritual growth and development.

I was born in 1963 and it's the same year Martin Luther King abolishes slavery in the Northern States.
John F Kennedy is shot dead.
Bob Marley gets a breakthrough. He's one of my first big idols.

As a child I was very sensing, sensitive and full of energy. I was probably a pretty happy child full of questions and monkey tricks. My child hood really was a good one, my father and mother took care of me and my siblings in a way the both of them found was for the best.

We didn´t lack of any materialistic things and we were kept healthy, clean and with full tummies and everything was fine and dandy.

Little Helena who wanted to be loved and get attention could have some of that if she was happy and positive. And so you learn pretty fast what works and what doesn´t work in the grownups world, as a child you adapt and take on an appearance to fit in.

I knew already from the beginning I was "different", that I heard and saw things the others didn´t and maybe that is why I tried even harder to appear plain and normal. I´ve made many regressions to heal and understand myself as a child. One of the first memories I came to in my regressions is a memory after my birth. It is of me lying in a cot. I know something terrible has happened and nothing will ever be like before.

My mother is gone. I don´t understand it at the time but physically she is dead. She will never again hold me in her arms, never cuddle me and say loving words to me, s*he is gone.*

The abandonment that comes upon me during the regression almost makes my heart burst and I see faces around me with a grief and anxiety. Maybe they are trying to hide what has happened but I know.

Well as you understand my mother dies. It´s nothing I can remember in my thoughts as I was too little at the time it happened. What I realized later was that there was a memory of this experience in my body to be healed.

Some of you souls have chosen this time to be borne into families and circumstances with different events and traumas along the way to awaken the old memory of who you are and why you are who you are and what your task is. This can be compared to you finding a dirty stone, which you polish just to find a fantastic crystal. The crystal is you and as layers of traumas, grief, fear, anger, old feelings and darkness from this life as well as earlier ones are cleared, you will arise in all your glory.
THE TRAUMAS, BETRAYALS, SORROWS, DISSAPOINTMENTS YOU HAVE CHOSEN ARE THE PASSAGE TO YOUR SOULS CRYSTAL. .
Dear children and collaborators! We are here to support and encourage you in your work with yourselves. Do not give up, the old resignation will too be brushed off from the crystal. When the code of your soul, your DNA sets the tone you will remember who you are and inside of you a force slumbers which now will awake.
We are with you on your journey. Have faith in yourself. Use your courage on the path when you meet and cleans this old darkness of fear, sorrow and anger. Soon your diamond will shine and glisten. When you set the tone in your DNA the memory of who you are and your inner journey to championship and perfection has begun.

The next memory is angels around my bed, big bright visions sending love and light to the little girl in bed, which is me.

I know my mother´s with these angels and grief and abandonment disappears when I in my solitude am with these light beings and my mother. Being alone now feels good, time

16

flies and as they say it also heals wounds. My father meets a new woman. She becomes my new mother. To be a happy and positive girl now becomes even more important and soon my baby brother is born.

Just like when my mother dies I know a new bigger change is approaching and I feel worried. I get anxious and think I will die every time I've injured or hurt myself.

My brother is born and now everything has to be perfect. My mother is obviously tired after pregnancy and childbirth and sometimes my grandmother, whom I love comes for a visit to help out.

During this time the dreadful happens in an instant. All brightness turns into a grey fog. I cannot speak with my mother in heaven anymore as we're supposed to be a whole family with our new brother.

The instant I'm told my throat chakra turns off and the grief being capped sets itself like a blocking in my throat. My parents of course think it's for the best. On the surface everything looks perfect.

Life goes on as per usual but inside I feel betrayed. There's a thorn in my heart difficult to forget, they have taken away one of the things that matters the most to me.

Drama

Your drama and spectacle will repeat itself until you understand and realize what it is all about. As we spoke of earlier all of you human children have a script and a drama reflecting what you want to learn and develop in this life.

This drama will draw your attention to what needs more light, to make it possible for you to heal and fill it with love and you will get inner peace. You have chosen a variety of basic blockings that can appear as imbalances in your chakras for you to evolve spiritually.

The chakras you have most commonly chosen as basic blockings are the three lower chakras: the Root chakra, the Sacral chakra and the Solar Plexus chakra.

If you have chosen basic blocking in your root chakra it can appear in many different ways for example shortage thinking. It can be a shortage of money or something else involving shortage, it can be different fears constantly recurring and a sense of insecurity. The sense of abandonment is linked here as well. The trauma usually occurs between 0 and 7 year of age.

Basic blocking in the Sacral Chakra can be expressed as feelings of guilt, depressions, abuse problems, assaults and abuse of power and a need to control. The trauma typically occurs between 7-14 years of age.

Basic blocking in the Solar plexus may manifest itself as inferiority complexes, low self-esteem, bad confidence and not being good enough and trying to overcompensate. Trauma usually occurs between 14-21 years of age.

These basic blockings are coded in your DNA as an imbalance and a blockage to develop and to teach you how to grow spiritually, mentally and physically

It is possible for you to dissolve these basic blockings yourselves by looking at and understanding them and then loosen up the energies holding the blockage, by for example healing, meditation or regressions.

These basic blockings can be followed like a red thread through the life you're living at the moment as well as going back to earlier lives. You could say they have similar themes.

According to Indian tradition we humans have seven different chakras we usually mention. These are situated at specific places on our body and are connected to one or several various functions and colours.

The Root chakra is connected to the red colour and the lower part of the body i.e. feet, legs, lower abdomen, kidneys and the bladder.

The Sacral chakra is connected to the orange colour and the lower part of the stomach, lumbar, hips, intestines and genitals.

The Solar plexus chakra is connected to the yellow colour and stomach, pancreatic, liver and the gall.

The Heart chakra is connected to the green or pink colour and to the heart and lungs.

The Throat chakra is connected to the blue colour and the thyroid.

The Third eye chakra is connected to the indigo blue colour and to the pineal gland as well as the third eye.

The Crown chakra is connected to the purple or white colour and is centred straight above the crown and represents the link between our spiritual, mental and physical body.

Healing with color

We would now like to give you information about colours and healing.

To us here in this dimension colours are of a strong frequency, having the ability to affect us deep down in our cells. Healing using colours is an excellent tool.

The red colour is as we mentioned earlier on, connected to the Root chakra and it vibrates slowly compared to the other colours. The red colour helps you to be more grounded and provides a safe and invigorating feeling.

You human children can use the red colour for starting up projects. It could be rehabilitating at exhaustion, to support transformation and to nourish love.

You human children are happy to use the red colour with your heart and you give red roses to the one you want to show your love.

The red colour is warming in its nature.

The blue colour is the opposite of the red one. It cools and sooths, cleans, harmonises, distances and helps you to clearer thoughts. It brings information about firmness and stability. The blue colour is connected to the throat and Throat chakra and gives support in communication and expressions.

Blue helps you letting go prior to the transition between the fourth and fifth dimension as well as prior to your physical death. It gives you the distance to your problems. The blue colour also provides healing in depth.

The purple colour, being a mixture of the red and the blue, has a high frequency affecting your spiritual vision and the third eye. This colour can be used to support your spiritual light bodies during for example healing work.
The purple colour brings promises of completion and rebirth and is good to use in processes of transformation. Purple will also help you in the transition from the fourth to the fifth dimension, i.e. you inner Peace journey.
With the help of meditation and arch angels and contact with the Pleiades, you will get perspective and new visions.

Much later in life I will come to the understanding I´ve chosen a basic blocking in the Root chakra but right here at this stage as a child I´m completely ignorant.

Animals and nature become what I seek out for instead, animals won't let me down. They love me just the way I am. I spend a lot of time in stables among horses. One day we get a horse in our family, I cheer with joy and I really love that horse. A feeling of being needed and that there is a meaning to my life again makes life good to live.

The animals

Animal are treated with respect and are given more space and love. They are appreciated for their specific properties and teach us about what we really already know. Honesty and naturalness.

Years passes by and one day our horse falls ill and dies. All the old pain from grief welling up again. It feels as if neither I nor anyone else understands the pain.

I pull away more and more and soon I move to another location to get an education. I harbour so much love within me and at the same time I thirst for it. I am now a young woman vibrating of light and life but pretty lost in existence.

To find love

To find love can sometimes feel difficult, yes sometimes almost impossible. We see from this dimension you look for it high and low. What you seek for in the outer, you all carry within.
If you could see and understand all the love you carry within you, you would also let it expand and by doing so easier draw forth the love you wish for and seek around you. Let the love for yourself expand. Love yourself and the beings of light that you are. You can seek in the outer indefinitely but if you do not take the step towards yourselves and see yourselves through the eyes of love and start loving the soul and the person you are without

the masks and perceptions or feeling you should be in a certain way to receive love, is a conception we from this dimension find awkward. It is as if an apple would transform into a pear. Can you hear how strange that sounds?

I start the education and there I meet friends at the adjacent adult education collage. I get especially good friends with one of the girls and we hang out through thick and thin.

One weekend we all go together to her parents place, we have a sleep over on matrasses in the so called library. We´re supposed to sleep but were fooling around like teenage girls do at that age. We are just about to fall asleep when I all of a sudden sense a presence and a dark cloak is laid over me. I can´t breathe or move. I can´t even scream and I lie paralyzed on the mattress thinking I´m going to die.

All of a sudden the pressure eases slightly and I scream out loud. I get up on the mattress and the fear gets even bigger as, together, we see a male figure sitting in one of the armchairs.

We dash out of the library and my girlfriend's mother comes running from her room. Pretty hysterical, we tell her what has happened. She listens calmly and then tells us it might have been a psychic experience.

She talks about being able to see the spirit world and I both understand and don´t understand. We move the mattresses to the adjoining room and I lie down next to the wall. My girlfriends fall asleep and I lie a long time waiting for sleep to come. Then all of a sudden the door to the room where we are opens without a sound and a bright woman figure turns up in the door smiling at me.

I fall asleep shortly after and think this might be one of my friend's sisters. Therefore I sleep safe and sound until the following morning and at breakfast the next morning I tell about the bright woman figure. My girlfriend looks puzzled and she says her sisters are neither in the house nor the village. I try to find an explanation but no one can answer my question.

The time that follows is a difficult time. I think I see and hear things which "are not there", it´s difficult finding someone to talk to about what has happened, so I shut it inside me. Shortly after this I get pregnant and choose to have an abortion as I´m not together with the father of the child.

After the abortion I feel even worse and I feel a fear of dying. A grey haze descends over me and my life. It´s difficult for me to talk about what has happened, but I´m on the edge as well of fear of "seeing" something which is not there, as I´ve learned to switch off, because it doesn´t exist.

Love

Love is a word to you earthlings which is, and is used for, many different things.
To us habitants of the Pleiades it is an energy.
A strongly vibrating energy containing a force unmeasurable to anything else.

*Love is the most powerful energy you human children have on
your earth.
Do not be so afraid of that power.
Many of you are afraid of the power of love and choose a
variety of other paths.
From this dimension it looks completely crazy, yes utmost in
sane. Sometimes you make large detours to avoid the wings of
love.*

*You choose loneliness and separation
You choose war
You choose drugs
You choose fear
You choose sorrow
You choose oppression
You choose power
You choose violence
You choose disease
The list can be made very long with everything you choose in the
darkness instead of love. We are telling you the time of love has
come and everything else you choose will slowly die.
Love is the force that in the end will be victorious in the war you
human children fight within and in the outer of your world.*

*We would like to encourage you to choose:
Love for yourself
Love for your children
Love for your next of kin
Love for the animals, nature and entire mother Earth*

*The love energy vibrates and gives gratitude extending into
infinity.*

*Choosing love is choosing life, peace on earth, health and a
bright future for the children, earth and universe.*
Love penetrates the tough shield that is meant to be peeled off.
*The shield will crack, fall off and then out of it you will be born,
you beautiful human children in the most beautiful colours and
radiant light vibrating of love, light and peace.*

We love you and send love, light and peace.

*Dear children, do not let anything stop you from reaching love.
Let all the blockings and fears become visible, for you to let go
of what is stopping you to feel and be in the energy of love.
Let all the old things die.*

Eventually the grey haze becomes thinner and lighter. I amuse
myself to forget about sorrows and to have more fun in my life.
I meet new friends and eventually I meet my husband, Stefan.

When I meet him my life take a drastic turn to the better on all
levels. All the love I´ve harbored can now run wild and I´m
overwhelmed with love right back. He loves me.

The meeting between people

*The ecstatic meeting between people is the fire that can light the
flame of passion. It is possible for you to see everything is
connected. The flame that lights up in your chest in your body is
also linked to your mission in life.*

Some of you have found that partner, where you together by the
meeting have lit that flame. We would like to encourage you to
seek for your soul mate, together the two of you can activate
that fire through the sexual meeting
And afterwards keep the flame alive with Love and the power of
friendship.
Give yourself that kindness and affection as well.

My husband and I discover common interests. These are nature,
animals as well as spiritual and occult areas. The year is now
1985 and we watch a program together on the television called
divining rod, pendulum and pointer. This is the starting point for
the both of us to use and learn more about divining rod,
pendulum and pointer. It sets off our common interest around
nature and the spiritual world. Eventually our first child is born.
A fantastic soul filled of light and love.

Children of the new Age

The children of the new age do not want to adjust to and accept
the guidelines, rules and laws which you have so stubbornly
maintained. The children of the new age wish to help you letting
go of old thoughts and values and help you see the beauty, the
love but also to let all stay as it is without manipulations and
adjustments to fit into the narrow minded society reflecting the
unwillingness of change and a so called male dominated way of
thinking. The so called feminine softness is subdued and thus
becomes submissive. The children of the new age come with the
flame of love in their chests and are not ready to give up until

you are awakened with an urge to make a transformation for the best of Earth and for man's peace with himself. The Chaos being created, is created to displace you from the old perception of what is good and what is evil, as these really do not exist but is a figment created by human. None of this exists in nature, but everything just is and nothing can compel the seasons or the growth. It all happens within their own development processes and cycles. To force something, either man or nature for financial gain will never help human or earth to peace and harmony but instead creates war, violence, depression and sorrows. See what you create, human children because you can create anything you like. You hold the key in your own hands. The children of the new age are radiant souls carrying the message of peace and love on Earth.

Associated to my pregnancy and labor, I now go through some physical and psychological problems. It makes me start seeing a woman for treatment, who is using different kinds of alternative methods. She helps me in a way nobody else has been able to. It is also the beginning of a rather intense period. I perceive and "see" souls from the spirit world. It is enforced with a tremendous power and I´m actually afraid I´m losing my mind.

As a newly become mother I´m very vulnerable. My fear of losing my mind along with my urge to imbed my experiences finally makes me discuss it with my husband. He looks at me and says he also felt a presence in the apartment where we are living. I cannot in words describe the ease spreading in my body from his answer and the inner knowledge of him also having felt the presence. We recognize it is obviously my mother visiting.

In retrospective I have also been told it is very common for us women to become more sensitive and sentient when we expect and give birth to children, as it comes naturally we are opening up for the new life being born.

The spirit world is now reopened in a way that makes me feel like coming home. I long for my visits to the woman. She tells me she can see me in the future working with alternative medicine and as a medium to help people. Her words become tiny seeds eventually growing into plants.

The flame of passion

When you do what makes your soul sing, your heart will laugh, know then you are on the right course with yourselves.
To feel joy, love and thankfulness is a gift more worth than any amount of money. To find your life's mission you should indulge in what brings you joy.
Out of the joy a song of thankfulness and love will grow. That is also the strong medicine bringing back life in what has stagnated and will help you heal. To find what gives you joy in your work and life is therefore of highest priority. This is one of the approaches in the new dimension, the fifth dimension.

1989 our second child is born and we name her Ronja. It´s a strong soul in a little body, an old and wise soul with love and light. And I know she was my mother in an earlier life.

The children and school

The children are freer and may from the beginning and during their first school years develop their special capabilities and talents they bring. They are encouraged and supported to be true to themselves and their inner voice.
Meditation is one of the main topics.
They will spend more time with animals and in nature.
Less bullying and injustice as it belongs in the fourth dimension. They are per definition darkness in its highest form.
In the fifth dimension there is an acceptance of differences and dissidents nourishing a freer and more conscious view on the human child.
The line between yours and mine is thinner and it is easier to share.
Gifts, generosity and voluntary work are corner stones in the school's development, as you now see the human child as a gift from the Gods and an investment in the future.
The wellbeing of the children is more IMPORTANT than money.

In the year of 1990 my husband and I set off to attend to our first healing course. It is an English healer called Matthew Manning. This marks the beginning of a big change. Our daughter Ronja is just over two years of age when she one day sits in the kitchen bench looking at me with her clear blue eyes. She asks the question straight out in the open.
- Mother, why are your eyes so sad?

The question hits me right in the heart because I don't even know the answer myself. How do you answer the question from a little girl who has just learned to talk and walk? This question triggered a process in my mind that would take a long time processing before it was over.

I think it´s sometime around now a bigger change starts within me. I start a three year long education in Chinese medicine. The spiritual journey sets off and many insights and understandings appears about who I am. Why certain things develop in a certain way and what patterns I´ve chosen on my life's journey.

All of this comes to the surface during my education. And it´s during this period I start realizing I possess psychic abilities I'm supposed to set free and develop. I start meditating regularly and it brings me an inner stability and force which I´ve missed. I now feel more alive than I´ve done in a long time. Life feels bright and full of hope.

At the same time I finish my education we move from our little three room apartment. We buy a small house on the countryside in the province of Skane. This is where we are going to stay. I will also start my business consisting of helping people through alternative medicine.

Moving to the house really feels like coming to a castle. A dream is being fulfilled. I´ve just about started and got going with my business. Then it happens what was not supposed to happen. I become ill.

A numbing fatigue which eventually turns into depression and anxiety. I see ordinary doctors and doctors practicing alternative medicine, but it´s difficult finding any cause to my disease. The ordinary medical profession takes a lot of tests just to find nothing. They finally put me on sick leave for depression and for being burnt out.

ℌospitals and other similar institutions

Hospitals are friendlier both in design as well as in reception.
To work there is a chosen task in life. Healing energies and
alternative medicines are natural elements and complements.
Relaxation, meditation and retreat is prescribed. .
The doctor and nurses have the knowledge to use healing
alongside other studies to help a person as a whole.
Emotions will be more in the center instead of symptoms.
The human is now looked upon as a whole. This is a holistic
approach.
Spirit, body and mind.

The different treatment methods can be chosen by yourselves
and never before throughout your history has it been this
beneficial for you to choose and affect what you want and wish
for.

We do not speak to you of what will become. It may become a
possible future if you break your old patterns of fear, sorrow
and control and anger. When you are now moving from the
fourth to the fifth dimension.
We are with you for support and encouragement from this
dimension.

Deep within I knew that to get help and to come back and be
healthy, I have to make my own journey. During a meditation I
get in contact with one of my spiritual helpers.

He hands me a sword telling me to accept it as a symbol, to use
it to "cut off" the shackles around my legs and feet. At first I
don´t understand what he means but he explains to me the

shackles are symbols of all of the fears I'm trapped in. A long
and painful process begins.

Healing

To receive healing and to become whole helps your body to self-
healing. There is a giving and receiving side in all humans,
female or male, Yin and Yang. To be healed you need to learn
how to receive. To receive belongs to your female side. Many of
you human children have difficulties in receiving without
controlling or analyzing. When you have the need to control you
block the healing energy that can heal and cure you. When
humankind has learned to be more receiving, a greater balance
is possible with yourself as well as with the earth. Meditation is
one of the keys to be able to receive. Do not try to control it but
simply receive whatever comes to you during the meditation.
In the history of mankind on earth the receiving side
(the female) has been mutilated, ridiculed, stomped on and
oppressed.
Now is the time to let the energies from this side of all of you
appear, helping mankind and earth to come to a balance making
it possible for both the female and male energies to become
whole.
We repeat meditation is one of the keys in receiving. The more
you receive of this life giving energy and the more you do
"nothing" the greater the possibilities are to help both
yourselves and mother earth.
Meditation is a method used by people in all times. To get in
contact with the God and Goddess this force was a tool you
used. Thousands of years ago when the female forces were more
prominent then today, mankind lived in more harmony and in

balance with the animals and nature. Look at indigenous people, the American Indians for example, they knew how to do just that. Today they are almost extinct and only fragments from ancient times are left. It is like this with all of those cultures, once thriving and living in balance. The female energies were revered and worshiped, as it is the female who is the life giving and nourishing.

It comes natural to me to seek help in the alternative medicine. I had a good experience and was helped by it before.

I get herbal medicine, healing, acupuncture and reflexology from a very good friend whom I´ve met during my education. From another good friend I got rebirth therapy. I meditate and rest, because I didn´t have much energy, but made my way slowly bit by bit.

Rest

To rest is important in times like these. Your cells are constantly being replaced and your physical body changes in its structure. Therefore to rest and letting yourself get extra sleep when you need is an act of love you can give yourselves when you are tired.
It is not ordinary times you are living in. It is a different era awaiting you and you are in the midst of a big transformation which the whole universe is a part of.
Rest, give yourself extra nourishment, love, support and encouragement. Nothing is wrong, everything is as it should be. Rest calmly and safely in trust.

34

All of the events led to what I didn't know at the time, the path towards peace with myself.

Slowly the picture emerged of the little girl Helena who felt abandoned, muted and betrayed. During a rebirth therapy session I get in contact with my dead mother. She gives me a symbolic peace dove.

I'm very deeply affected by the incident and carry it with me in my heart. I also get connected to previous lives and see myself as a shaman from Greenland where my friends are the wild animals, such as killer whales, polar bears and seals.

Even though I don't feel well, the connection with previous lives and the contact with my mother, gives me strength in a strange kind of way.

In the time that follows I find it very difficult to move forward. The paralyzing fatigue haunting me. I'm constantly dizzy as well and I carry a profound fear my beloved husband will leave me, now when I'm ill. Deep within me is the fear of being abandoned, the fear I've carried since my mother died.

It's at this time during a therapy session I realize I need to heal the grief of my mother, by mourning her. This is to be able to let go of the fear of being abandoned as well. I don't have a living memory of my mother's death but understand there is a memory in my body of grief. The sadness my darling daughter has reminded me of.

I decide to look up my mother's grave. I'm encountered with the news it no longer exists. Initially it makes me feel sad, but instead I create a place to where I can go and honor her memory and allow myself to mourn. This is probably more of a symbolic grave, but at that moment this is important to me.

It´s not easy to start rummaging in my past. It gives me deep anxiety. But amidst the anxiety there is also a profound gratitude being able to allow myself to heal. The hardest part is the feeling I´m not good enough and that I don´t have enough strength to cope with our three children.
In a way it feels like I´m abandoning them in my disease. I´m depressed and burdened with feelings of guilt. I´m certainly not feeling particularly well at this point.

Deep inside however, I knew my recovery was in allowing myself the grief in order to let it go.
I´ve been to the doctor´s and had tests made on the thyroid gland.
I get the test results for a third time. The test results indicate an underactive thyroid gland.

This is of course both a relief and a sorrow as it is liberating to know everything I´ve been going through is not only due to psychological imbalance, but also due to a hormonal imbalance of my body.

I try to learn as much as possible about problems of the thyroid gland. I realize it´s mostly women who suffer from the problem, about 90% which is quite interesting.
I put a lot of thoughts into this. Could it be because women are more often holding back? And because girls in general should be nice and quiet while boys are allowed to be more noisy and rowdy?

I recognize myself in what I find. I cry with relief when I understand there´s a way out of this dark tunnel. I see the connection between a disabled Throat chakra and my disease and I decide to heal it at the root. I want to go the bottom of the disease.

To let go

To let go might be something bringing you sorrow. It can be an event forcing you to let go or something suddenly being taken away from you. Your entire physical being and soul can assist you in letting go.

To breathe and make your breathing a part of your everyday life is now very important. Breathing, breath, is also a way for you to connect with your own spirit. Your spirit and your breath is in constant contact with the air and the universe and through information from your spirit and universe, you will find it easier to know how to let go.

Allow the grief which is stored. This is a sign you are now letting go. Your whole being is helping and notifying you of what you are finding yourself in, now that you are letting go. In nature, on your earth there is a natural rhythm of letting go. In your DNA, your cell memory there is information about when and how you can let go. You activate this through your breathing and meditation. Have faith and trust and know that you are protected and loved as you were when you were born to this earthly life.

The pain and the sorrow is a part of the process of letting go, just like when we are born. Difficult, tedious, hard to breathe, dark, narrow and horrific but still you can do it. Beloved children, we love you and out of the womb of the vast universe

you are now being born. Your mother is the earth and your
father the universe and we are assistants in this great event. In
the beginning you might be small and fragile but with
nourishment and love you will grow to be strong.

As an answer to my wish for help I get in contact with a
wonderful woman. She works with Gestalt therapy and Jungian
psychotherapy. Nothing happens as a coincident but rather
things come our way when we're open to them.

So I start participating in something called Gestalt therapy. I do
this for a while, both in a group and individually with her.

During the therapy I get insights and come to the understanding
little Helena has been silenced both by herself out of fear of
being abandoned again, as well as by the surroundings and thus
the Throat chakra has been blocked. I`m helped by the woman/
therapist and a period of deep healing follows.

Heal your inner child

Your inner child is crying, hear how it calls out for you.
It seeks comfort, nourishment and attention.
Continually the child does things to be noticed.
- Speaks about how important she is, what she can and will do.
-Wants to be seen and heard.
-Is afraid of different things and prevents itself from doing what
would be good for it.
Yes the child creates all kinds of situations because it needs
support, healing and understanding. We spoke of before your

earlier lives and how at this moment, there is like a symbolic funnel from the fourth to the fifth dimension and everything old must pass through the funnel to be sorted. A rebirth awaits you. It is a higher vibration, love vibration which you are being born into, so that your inner child can heal.
All of the old must die to allow the new to be born

For those of you who have already undergone the transformation from the fourth to the fifth dimension, the energy from us is even closer and telepathic transmission from us to you and vice versa is now even easier.

One could say you are getting closer to your own divinity, the divine, the Goddess and the God you have within.
Some of you are guides, mediators, midwives or historians in this galactic adventure.

Dear human child and friend, we see your work and wish to support and enforce each and every one of you.

We look upon you as points of light which gradually, as you let go of the coat of darkness from earlier lives and this life, will expand and become pillars of light reaching out to animals, nature and mother earth.
Beautiful human children, we love you and send you love, light and peace to the planet.

I´m determined to get well and with a lot of stubbornness, help and support from therapy and the family, slowly but surely I recover. It´s not an easy journey but in my heart I'm determined to go to the bottom with the cause of my disease in order to get well.

During the same period of time my husband participates in an education to become a regression therapist. He´s found an advert in a paper about the education. It´s a woman holding it. It´s the beginning of our friendship with this woman and we will see more of her and her husband in the future.

After the course he returns full of all the amazing past lives he has experienced.

And following this, he guides me through a series of regressions. We do this to see if there is something from past lives affecting the throat and the Throat chakra and my problem with the Thyroid gland.

In one the lives I come to, I´m living in Egypt. I´m a woman and Stefan is my husband in this life as well. I experience I´m taken prisoner and locked up and strangled in a pyramid. Someone has hired guards to kill me as I´m uncomfortable and working with helping and guiding other people. I´m a so called wise woman. In this life I tell "truths" and use my power to "see". This is what is bothering the man who wants to kill me.

I die inside the pyramid. The sense of strangulation and sadness disappears and I cry with relief. Naturally this is connected to my shut Throat chakra.

One of the insights following that journey is in order to become whole, I also need to let my psychic abilities emerge even more.

In this past life I´m killed for having used my wisdom and my inner seeing, the medial ability.
But I´m also punished and killed because of it. Unconsciously I´ve been holding myself back both of fear of saying something

that cannot be said, but also from the fear of being punished and killed.
To use my Throat chakra and communicating my feelings and to access the force. To speak from my heart will help me remove the blockage making me ill.
Bits and pieces are falling into place and I get a new platform to stand on. Slowly I return to life.

We now speak to you of past lives

You are all souls on a journey through the lives, the lives you yourselves have ones chosen to experience and learn from.
In the times you are now living the lives accumulate as in a funnel to be sorted, looked upon and to help you letting go of old patterns like for example anger, sorrow, control. The funnel can be compared to a channel of birth into the new age. We know it can be a struggle to be born but prior to birth there is also a death.
Everything old you have been carrying as burdens will die. It has been holding your viability back.
Imagine the gold mine you hold in your hand. All the lives you have lived putting you through rigours, lessons of life, insights and knowledge. You now have access to all of this. Set off on a breath-taking journey back in time and study your own spectacle and drama.
Dear human children now is the time to put on your own birth costume.
Faith and trust will help you on the path.

I slowly get back to my work again and have a steady flow of customers coming to see me. They come with all kinds of problems and I help them through conversation, acupuncture and guidance. I´m pleased with my life and I´m doing smaller meditation groups and séances as well.

ℳeditation

Meditate. Slow down the speed, and look inwards, and you will speed up your own and the earths development. When you help yourselves through meditation, you help your children, fellow humans, animals and mother earth as well.
We believe meditation in different forms should be a major subject in all of your schools, work places and in homes.
To work towards this is something we warmly wish to support. Your children are carriers of the light in the future, help them find their inner path so that they will know how and where to, they are going to create paradise for themselves and the earth. Many of your children are very old souls. It is very difficult for them to return to earth. Therefore they need extra support and help in finding their lives assignments, bringing their souls peace, balance and happiness.
Happiness is a word which you think can be bought for money, but happiness lives WITHIN you. You just need to open the door, the door to your heart and follow that path. The path to your heart is love. To seek love within, in your next of kin, the animals and nature is the path to find happiness.
Help your beloved child to see itself as the wonderful divine presence it is. In that way you will help them find their own happiness.

You know all of this already, we would just like to remind you to
take that step towards a new dimension and raise yourselves
and earth to a new frequency, namely the frequency of love
vibrating with love, understanding, forgiveness and happiness.
Let go of old feelings!
Your drama will repeat itself until you have understood!
Meditation, meditation, meditation.
So simple, so obvious, but yet so difficult for you while you are
running.
Stop running after dead things, make a halt now!
Do not wait any longer, your mother earth is slowly dying
beneath your feet.
Many of you will gather to support and raise the energy.
We blow a fanfare to the universe and a wave of ecstasy will be
returned to you.

On September 11 in 2001 one of the first most upsetting
happenings in a long time takes place. It´s the World trade
centre being destroyed in an air attack. It is said that World trade
centre could be a symbol of the male energy in the shape of two
phallus symbols.

In certain quarters it´s also said it´s a symbol for the strong
female energies getting closer and closer to earth. This would be
the start.

In retrospect we know more disasters will follow. But we are not
aware of them at the time.

As the amount of people seeking my help increases I eventually
decide to rent bigger premises in a close by village. In the same
period of time I go to another city holding séances.

Here I receive the first messages of peace. In one of the séances Sitting Bull is appearing. He comes with messages of peace. As I don´t even know who he is, I initially think of it as a fun thing. At the same time, there are channelled messages from a big light essence. It´s information about the Pleiades, the so called 7 sisters. I really haven´t the faintest idea what the Pleiades are. Eventually this message falls into oblivion.

With time the messages from Sitting Bull increase and there is also another north American Indian by the name of Sitting Bear. They come with messages of peace. This is one of the messages and the year is now 2003.

It is time! Make haste!

Your children are crying and you need to hear them!
Not just your own children, but all children, even the child inside you!
They cry with the reason they cannot be who they are,
but they are imprisoned and strangled in their development.
You know all of this,, but maybe you do not wish to see or hear.
To make peace possible, make peace with yourselves.
Look within!
In order to have peace in your hearts, cry!
Feel your yearning!
Become who you are!

You are spiritual beings created by the mother on earth and the father in the sky.
Unite the two of them inside you!
All is one.

You take from your earth, you plunder it, steal with greed and think there is a shortage.

You impoverish the soil.
Put your chest against Mother earth and feel the heartbeats!
Raise your gaze towards the sky and receive the light!
Pray and unite with each other!
Make a chain, make a chain so strong, no one can break it!
Together you are strong!
Together you become whole!

Walk into the silence!
Silence says more than thousand words!
Walk in stillness with yourselves!
You know the answers, you receive the answers, you have the answers.
Listen to your heart which has not yet stopped beating!
Live out your yearning!
Live out your love!

I would like you to contemplate what I have said.
Contemplate if you wish...
It is not up to me.
It is up to you.
You hold it in your hand.
All you have been given.
It seems you take the gifts from earth for granted.

I wish to hand over a pipe of peace.
Take it to your hearts!

It is only you who can decide if you would like to take it.
It is your own choice, how you choose to act.

Do not feel any weight on your shoulders. You put it there
yourselves.
You can take the weight away.
Make your own decision!

What is to control your actions?
Is it the love you yearn for
or is it the fear?
Make peace with your fear!
Make peace and open up to love!
Be like a bird and fly!
Wherever you want, how you want, when you want.
You were given wings to fly.
There is more to be said but it is enough for now.
Contemplate what I have said
WALK IN PEACE!

Sitting Bull

These are strong messages and must be taken seriously.
I don´t know as yet what to do with these messages.

Several years later I receive the first messages from the Pleiades.
And I hear in my mind they are also messages of peace.
These messages are to be written and mediated to other people
as a help in the transition to the new age.

46

To open your channel

Open your channels so that the light we send together with the messages for you, will spread like a wave in the new net of energy now being formed on mother earth.
With meditation, contemplation, love power and healing and through contact with other channels of light you can activate the channel present in each and every one of you.
This channel has been present since the beginning of time and can be compared to a socket and a cord now being connected. Now the lamp, which is you, can be lit and the enlightenment passing over earth from other dimensions will help you see the darkness and to remove everything old being stagnated, blocked and steeling energy from the earth and you earthlings.

At Christmas Eve 2004 a big ring is seen around the moon and two days later the tsunami appears in Thailand. It's a very shattering experience too many people.
The world will never be quite the same after this happening.
Is this ring around the moon two days earlier, a prediction of what was about to happened? What we know in retrospective is this catastrophe will be followed by many more catastrophes around the world.

At the same time period and associated to the séances, we come in contact with a woman telling about Crete. She talks about a place on the southwest part of the island called Paleochora. There are dolphins and it's a wonderful place to be. This sets a little seed in us which slowly grows.
The winter of 2004 we decide to take the whole family to Crete and we arrive first of May 2005. We will be sunbathing,

swimming and resting and just spend time together. It feels wonderful

During a part of our stay, my husband will attend to a course including how to use a divining rod. After looking at the map we realize that in this heat, it is too far taking the kids to Paleochora and the wild dolphins.
So we decide hopefully we can go there another time. And much later we will get there.

My husband spends the days on the divine rod course and I go swimming and sun bathing with the kids.

During an excursion I get a picture in my mind that the meridians on our bodies are connected further out in the universe and further to the stars. I discuss it with my husband and afterwards it falls into oblivion. This little episode should prove to be of greater importance further on, but I´m not aware of it at the time.
Time passes and one day an old girlfriend invites me to her house. It´s a sweet little townhouse and she likes me to see it. She tells me she´s going to finish refurbishing it and after that enjoy her home and says now she will live there for the rest of her life.

I go to her house and we sit talking. My eyes are drawn to a small brochure lying on a table. I ask if I can take a look and of course I can. It´s about flowers and flower therapy. It´s a woman in Denmark who manufactures flower essences.
My friend says she will attend to the education starting this autumn. I´ve both used flower essences and made some essences of my own just for the fun of it.
This makes me familiar with the therapy.

Flowers and plants

*Flowers and plants are carriers of divine energies and reflect a
micro cosmos.*

*And you also know when the flower gets nutrition it develops
and you can make use of that energy through various processes.*

*Right from the beginning of your time, mankind have understood
the healing power of plants, flowers and herbs.*

*To get the finest and most pure energy from the plant and flower
it can be put in water to let the sun, moon or some other source
of energy infuse it with light.*

*You are aware of, when different things are emerged, new forms
are created. It is MAGIC. With the help of water, a flower and
light a healing essence emerges and it enters your body at a
cellular level and vibrates to make you more coherent with your
higher self.*

Thus it is also a tool on your path to inner peace.

I recall the first time I used flower remedies. It´s many years ago
when our children were small and their baby brother were born.
He´s an old soul of light and love.

The two oldest children who have been friends through thick
and thin are starting to fall out. As a parent you feel heartbroken
and don´t know what to do. At the child care centre I´m advised
to give more attention to and activate the older children.

With a newly born toddler on my arm I try to. I give our
children attention and try doing different activities with them.
But it makes no difference.

Then I´m recommended through a good friend working as a
Biopath to use a flower remedy called holly. This is to prevent
jealousy.

After using the essence for a week the children are friends again. I´m deeply impressed by the power contained in the little bottle. This memory together with the education are being mixed and I feel a forceful chill along my spine.

This makes me completely convinced I´m also going to join that education. I contact the woman in Denmark holding the course and it turns out there´s a spot left for me.

Meetings

In every meeting between people there is a change of vibrations. Two different energies meet and in some meetings there is a consonance. In other meetings there is a dissonance.
Trust your feel when there is consonance!
These people might have crossed your way for a special reason. Sometimes maybe for a smaller reason and sometimes for a larger.
When you meet a soul mate and partner for life a consonance appears and when your bodies meet there is a magical vibration unique for the two of you. In the meeting new energies emerge and new forms and sometimes even pure physical life.
Through the union your bodies and souls can communicate on an earthly as well as spiritual plane.
Together you open up for new dimensions and in what you human children call an orgasm a union of the divine is taking place, between the universal God and Goddess.
In devotion and ecstasy, right there is where the meeting takes place and in that meeting there is a very special magic you people like to access.

We would like you to bring down the ecstasy to an earthly plane. Therefore it is very important you try feeling devotion and ecstasy in your life's work.
Precisely there is where it is possible for you to bring down the devotion and ecstasy through your spirit and mind and let it take a physical form in your body.
Your body is your instrument to reach heights you never thought possible. By loosening blockages and traumas which has taken a physical form in your body, you will achieve a free flow.
This is made possible through your channel and body.
We wish to encourage the free flow through your body. Use your creativity, happiness and desire and let miracles come into your life.

An intense development sets off and with the help of these wonderful flower essences we are assisted in our own healing process.

It's like peeling an onion. Layers of old feelings from both this and past lives are slowly dissolved through the flower drops. This is combined with healing and conversations.
At the same time I realize the feelings of sorrow, resignation and anger was linked at the depth to the problems with my throat and the Thyroid gland. Now these blockages are released. I become whole and healed in my feelings.

This marvellous woman becomes my mentor and teacher and a very strong road model to me in the continuance of my spiritual work.

The same winter I started my education a dream reappears. In the dream I'm told from the spirit world to make essences of my

own. These essences are to be made in a specific manner, they are to be made on crop circles.
At first I think it sounds a little odd. The dream reappears and finally I tell my husband about it. He´s obviously all fired up with enthusiasm.

I don´t know much about crop circles. But with time I understand it´s better the less I know, because then I enter the process with no preconceptions.
My husband has been interested in crop circles for a very long time. So the dream about making crop circle essences repeating itself to me, makes the whole of him light up.

This makes us decide to jointly proceed with the idea of making flower essences. We´re wondering whether someone has done this before. We search the internet but can´t find anything. It feels exciting to make the essences and we are looking forward to it.

𝕯ear Human children

Use your feel, playfulness and what you refer to as fantasy when you are contacting us.
What you human children call fantasy are threads of light vibrating from your body out in the universe. This net spreads further out into the universe and you can receive information through what you call fantasy. The word fantasy may sound like something imaginary to you. Remember then, the chair you are sitting on or the car you are driving actually once were make-believe. Some of you find it easier than others, letting these

threads reach out in universe but through practice and
meditation everyone can stretch them further and further out.
On these threads you can also travel with your higher self. If
you wish, it is possible for you to physically manifest the
information you pick up during these journeys.
The word make-believe can be sectioned into the two words
make and believe, i.e. something you make when you believe.
Use your sense of humour and play with the words!
Exercise your visual ability and use different colours, shapes
and symbols. These constitute the universal language.

And then comes the night when we will make the essences.
There has been medial instructions they are to be made during
the full moon in a so called peace ceremony. There are clear and
distinct directives and I´m supposed to be used as a channel to
receive messages about the essences and the significance of
them. The overall significance is to help us create more peace
with ourselves and to our earth.

We understand the importance of us participating together to
keep the male and female energies in balance.
If we can achieve more balance between our male and female
energies in ourselves, it will be helpful in the process of
restoring the balance on our mother earth.

It´s a very special night and the full moon is high in the sky. In
the horizon there is thunder and lightning. We sit in the night
under the light of the full moon watching the spectacle in
silence.
All of a sudden, both of us see something which we at first think
is a satellite moving fast across the firmament. Suddenly the
light ball comes to a halt right above us. The light turns down

towards us and like a lamp with a strong light it beams down over us. Then all of a sudden it´s gone. What was it?

A strong shiver runs through the both of us and it feels as if someone from above wanted to say or show us something. The feeling the event is linked to the essences we´re making, cannot be mistaken. It´s a powerful feeling and a new baby is born, the Essence of Inner Peace.

Crop circles

What you human children refer to as crop circles are communication and messages from us here on the Pleiades. Myths have raised and different movements have formed on your earth to find an explanation to the formations of peace messages we send you.

We know these formations affect you in the depth and down to a cellular level, down to your DNA. You make tests and take samples and we know many of you already bear the knowledge of this. You can use these pictures and symbols in several different ways. And by using them you spread the messages of peace on your earth.

We wish to encourage you to use and spread the symbols in different ways.

The symbols carry various frequencies and affects your chakras. To many people it is a very big event to get in contact with and even to be standing in them. We look upon you as children who have found something exciting but you do not quite understand what it is. Use your curiosity and put trust in your feel during the contact with the symbols. The symbols and the messages are increasing as we are energetically getting closer to each other.

You will see new formations even on places where they haven´t been before.
Attention in what you people refer to as media will allow more human children to be aware of these crop circles. By using balls of light we telepathically send the information which then creates the forms and messages – crop circles.

Pictures of Crop circles in the south of England.

Some of you already understand the messages they carry and you are one of them. We see the work you and your husband are doing and we rejoice with the success. The messages are now to be spread out to larger groups and you are pillars of light in the dark.

Beautiful human children, we love you and would like you to feel joy, happiness, love, peace and light. Together you can make astral journeys to our dimension and charge yourselves with power to continue your work.

During the spring we´re going to the woman who´s educated Stefan in regression therapy. We´re taking a course with her husband Arne Groth. The course is about trauma circles but also about frequency stairs which he has discovered. Arne is very well known in the circuits of people using divining rod.

We regard it as a mini holiday and an opportunity for us to learn more about the things we´re interested in.

Arne has become of age and is rather tired, making him fall asleep in between sentences during his lecture.
Those are very special days we have together. We laugh quit a lot as in the midst of the seriousness, many comic situations occur.

After measuring out each other's trauma circles, eventually we all join in to help one of the men in the course.
As we measure out where the man´s trauma circles are located, I have a visual picture of a younger woman who seems to be in the man's energy field.
I tell the man about what I experience and at first he looks confused but after a while he lights up. Yes, he thinks he knows the woman from the description I give him. It´s an old love from his youth.

But what is she doing in his aura and energy field? I take another look and I see she´s there because he never let go, due to unrequited love, which he confirms.
We help him by removing her from his aura and he feels alert in a way he can´t explain.

This is the event which later develops into the method of energy thieves.

It´s not just Arne being tired because the rest of us are almost falling asleep as well, sitting in the sofa. We start discussing this and I get a picture of two men from the other side.
One of them turns out to be Arne´s father coming for a visit and he has a small message for Arne. The other man is of an older model and sits on a horse. He has a uniform with shiny buttons and a sabre in hand.

I don´t get the time to say any more about it, before someone says to Arne there is an unwanted presence in the room. Arne then grabs his crutch and makes a magical move sweeping through the room. He mumbles something like "here will not be any disturbing energies". He sweeps up the unwanted energy and literally throws it out the window.

The sofa in Arne´s home with the unwanted energies. Do the light balls and veils belong to Charles XII and Arne´s father?

A calm settles in the room and we continue our teaching.

A little later on in the afternoon, Arne calls me and wants me to join him to his room to find something that came to his mind and which he would like to show us.

It's pretty messy in the room and normally he doesn't let anyone else in, but apparently I get an exemption. He walks around searching through the mess and my eyes get stuck on a picture above the desk. It's of a man sitting on a horse. He wears a uniform with shiny buttons and a sabre at hand.

At that instant Arne finds what he's looking for and starts talking about it and we go downstairs to join the others.

After dinner the same night I sit talking with his wife and come to think of the picture in Arne's room again. I ask her if she knows who it is and she replies that it's Charles XII and it's the big idol of Arne's.

I tell her about the incident with Arne when he threw the unwanted energies out through the window. We get a good and long laugh from the crazy history as we realize Arne tossed Charles XII out the window using his crutch.

Humour, happiness and laughter

When you laugh and rejoice your souls get wings and the energies flowing through your bodies flows to your aura as well and creates rings of happiness. Happiness is the song from the fifth dimension. Therefore to laugh and rejoice is another tool helping you forward to the fifth dimension. Humour is a gift, given you to use. To laugh at yourselves, to see the humoristic side of a situation and to rejoice with family and friends, yes everything making you happy will raise you to the fifth dimension. Let happiness be the guide in moments of darkness and doubts.

A few months later Arne´s wife calls to tell us Arne died and moved on to the other side We feel a big grief about the fact Arne has left us but know in our hearts he´s with us from the other side. The story about Charles XII still makes us laugh.

The same summer we go for a mini vacation and rent a little cabin in the woods. We´re out hiking in the wood and at night when we return, Stefan doesn´t feel well. He´s dizzy and feels a little nauseous. We discover he carries a small essence "tagging" along. It´s a little Deva, a nature spirit which settled on his Third eye chakra. She has a message. She tells us the nature spirits seek our help. They need help debugging all the telephone masts.

They ask us to put visual protection in the shape of pillars of light around the masts when we see them. She tells us the masts disrupt the energies in nature and the invisible lines running around earth like a net. Those lines help earth, animal and nature.
We do know animals nesting close to these masts breed malformed and dead pets. So we promise to help out with this mission and I think we planted more than 100 pillars of light on the way home from the cabin we rented.

Nature and its essences

In your beautiful nature there are essences and beings wanting to support and help you in achieving more balance on earth. Maybe you cannot see these beings with your bare eyes. In native cultures and amongst native people one can see them. They knew everything possess a soul.
We would like you to reconnect with these essences of nature. They are in need of your help but would also like to be of assistance with the great net of energy now building up for the fifth dimension.
We see you still have some essences in your culture. Gnomes and trolls we would give the term beings of nature. Other essences which in a way can be compared to us habitants of the Pleiades are devas and fairies. Those are more of ethereal nature and assists flowers and plants and the energy grid linked to them. Many beings would now like to reconnect with you human children. Listen carefully and spend time in nature, and you will connect.

One day my husband comes with the suggestion we should buy a house in the village to run our business. He´s found an old house on the internet which no one else seems interested of. We get to buy the house at a good price.

We renovate, paint and put up new wall papers and finally we are as good as done. The courses and the treatments I give becomes more and more.

I teach energy medicine, psychic development, meditations and in addition I´m doing private seating's and treatments.

I´m offered to give massages on a company in a city some miles away. All of this gives us the opportunity to pay the mortgage on the house. Everything is looking bright.

Two years later when I go the city to do my massage job, I get a notice the company is going through a reorganization. They no longer need my services. The notice hits like a bomb and I only get until the end of the month to finish my work.

We´re now forced to sell the house where we run our business. But the thoughts of there being a reason for what is happening follows me.

With this in mind a new vision takes its form. If we sell both of our houses the dream of a farmhouse in the country can come true. Since the day we met we´ve had a joint dream of a farm house in the country side.

One day I get the idea I will go tanning in a solarium. This is something I nearly never do, but I feel I´m low in energy and I´m thinking the light might cheer me up.
On my way there I spot a newly opened real estate firm advertising house objects in the window.

My eyes are drawn to a farm and my feel tells me we´re going there to have a look. Someone or something has been urging me to go there, to make us see the farm.
Well at home we decide to pay the farm a visit. We go there to have a look and immediately we understand this is the place for us to live and develop our business.

Thanks to me losing the massage job and the house we´ve refurbished, we can now live the dream of a farmhouse in the countryside.

Have faith in yourselves

Faith is a word carrying strength and power. To have faith in something and yourselves will help you getting through times of confusion, darkness and fear more quickly. Look upon faith as a tool to hold on to in stormy weather or a safe hand to hold on to when you feel fear. What you believe in is not important, more important is you carry the faith in your heart. Believe there is a purpose in life, believe there is a purpose with your life´s journey, believe you are protected, and believe in yourselves. Faith gives direction, meaning and strength to be true to yourselves and your inner voice. This is a path we wish to encourage.

In August the house where we run our business is sold and we decide to take a vacation. We find a flight to Cyprus.

The whole family goes on holiday for swimming, sunbathing and to gather new energy.
We land in stifling heat and the first days we don´t have the energy to do particularly much.

One of the days when we went out to have dinner on a close by restaurant a strange thing happens.
Our daughter had previously been in an accident and sustained a neck injury. She complains about her aching neck. Suddenly she

asks if we can call for Arne from the other side and ask him for help.

In silence we ask to get in contact with Arne, both as a fun thing but half seriously as well. With my medial sense I see him coming and he stands behind our daughter and starts pulling out strange things from her neck and back. I communicate medially with him and ask what it is and he replies there is so much garbage from all around, nobody knows where it comes from.

He keeps doing it for a while and then he disappears. It seems our daughters' neck feels better and we order in some food.

We eat and enjoy ourselves when in the corner of my eye I see a man entering the restaurant. He looks strikingly like Arne but it isn´t him. I give my husband a quick push and whisper to the others what I see. I think we all sit with long faces as we notice the similarities between that man and Arne.

As we walk back to the hotel and go to bed that night we´re probably wondering a little bit what it is all about.

Before we left for our journey my husband was in contact with Arnes' wife and got information about a place on the island where Arne had been earlier to ”debug” a line, which were said to affect the Solar plexus chakra and was the cause of conflicts. It´s a so called minus two line.

That information is contained in the back of the head and it feels as if we´re supposed to go to the castle where this line has been ”debugged” with the help from Arne. It´s still very warm but we decide to rent a car following day and go to the castle.

We arrive during the day and it´s hot. It makes it even more pleasant staying inside the castle which is cool and a little damp.

I almost instantly feel the contact from Arne and he gives instructions of a stone-like thing in the basement of the castle, placed under a meter high pillar. He´s urging us to take the thing and throw it into the sea.
The floor is completely clean and my husband and the boys lifts the pillar and indeed, there lies some kind of stone. We take it and quietly put the big pillar back.

I hear Arne urging us again to throw it in the sea.
We leave the castle to do so. It´s very warm but we get in our rented car and set off on our mission.

Now a series of incidents occurs, making it difficult for us to reach the sea.
Horses are loose on the road. Trucks and excavator tractors are blocking the road and we have to turn around several times to find another way to the sea.

Finally we get there and can throw the thing in the sea and a sense of relief spreads among us. Now we´re hungry and we go looking for a place to have a meal. We finally find a place and we go inside to order a bite to eat. There is just one more party in the restaurant.
We sit down.

After a long time the waiter comes to take our order. He looks angry and seems to be in a grumpy mood. Strange as he was just previously joking around with the other party.
We place our order and finally get our food, one at a time and with long intervals. Every time he comes to our table he is

grumpy. In between he seems happy and he´s joking with the other party.

We begin to suspect his behaviour has something to do with us just tossing the stone-like thing in the water.

After this incident we feel a strong need of getting rid of negative energies and we decide to drive to the cliff of Aphrodite. We can go for a swim here and cleans off these negative energies.

After this event we have a peaceful and lovely holiday.

Is this Arne in the middle?

Means of transportation

As means of transportation you will not use petrol driven cars or vehicles in the fifth dimension.
The government and state will provide grants to make it possible for people to invest in Air cars and Water cars. Petrol is only used exceptionally.
Even homes and companies now use more environmental friendly options as heat sources.
The government suggests introduction of taxes on non-environmental friendly heat sources.
There are more discussions of what is good for earth in long terms and bigger focus is put into sustainability and what is nature-friendly.

Three days before Christmas Eve 2007 we move to the farm. On Christmas Eve we notice so called "orbs" in photographs taken in the room where we were celebrating Christmas.

On such an old farm there can be a lot of energies and spirits.

We repair and arrange, but for some reason the kitchen never feels quite right. No matter what we do there is a heavy feel to it

66

and we realize there is someone or something from the spirit world disturbing.

We hold a family séance and get in contact with a woman who says she used to live on the farm. Her little child has passed away and she carries a grief leaving an energy print on the kitchen. We help her and her little child to cross over to the light and the feel of the kitchen becomes lighter.

That same summer my husband and I are going to a medial demonstration. The woman holding it has through help from the spirit world been drawing some portraits to which she has received associated texts as well. She shows us the pictures, reading the texts with the hope someone will recognise the persons on the pictures and understand the texts.
She holds up a picture of a man and reeds the text. The room is silent and nobody seems to recognise him. We recognise what she is reading but not the man in the picture.

The result of the demonstration is that we go home with a picture of a man we don´t know. We don't have the faintest idea of who he might be.

One day my husband sits by the computer. A thought appears we got some pictures of the farm when we bought it. He finds the pictures and at the same time he remembers the picture we brought home after the séance. Ha calls for me to find it. Yes, there he is, the man we got at the séance. We put the photograph and drawing next to each other and find they are identical!

Now we become really curious and so we try to find out who the man really is.

My husband runs over to the neighbouring farm with the picture and he finds out the man is one of the previous owners of the farm.

That same summer there is a knock on the door and my husband opens. Outside is a woman in her forties and as she introduces herself says she used to live on the farm and would like to pay a visit to see who we are.
After a while of conversation my husband thinks of getting the picture of the man we received at the séance. The woman immediately recognizes him and says it´s her grandfather.
She tells us more about him and also confirms her grandmother lost the little child, just as we found out during our family séance. A secure feel comes over us and we understand some of the previous owners of the farm back in time, are keeping a watchful eye on us and helping us with the farm.

In the spring of 2008 I receive a new telepathic message from the Pleiades.

There are instructions of developing seven journeys to the Greek islands and finding seven places connected to the chakra points. These chakra points were supposed to be energetically connected to the Pleiades.
The points were to be activated by staying there during meditation and some kind of ritual.

Cellular memory and DNA were to be activated and revive old
memories of the roots of our true self and to find the inner
Goddess. The memories were to be linked to the time of Atlantis
existence. In that age the female and male force were in balance
with each other.

A visual picture shows where these chakra points are situated
and I ask my husband for help to see if the points can be
matched with the constellation of the Pleiades.
We twist and turn and finally we almost get it together. We´re
thinking about and trying to find out why it´s not quit matching?
And the answer appears, it´s because the earth has moved, but
the energetic bond between the points and the Pleiades is still
there.
Now we just need to find the points in reality. I realize we´ve
already found five of the points.
There is still two to be found.

We decide to search out these points on the journey we´re taking
to Crete during the autumn.

One of the points we find are for the Throat chakra. There are
clear medial instructions of whereabouts the point should be and
we take out a map to find it. In one of the séances I´ve held there
has also been a message that the point for the Throat chakra is in
an insignificant place.
On that place yellow flowers will be growing.

It´s warm and we set off out into a mountainous and arid
landscape. We know the point is on an ancient monument but
it´s not that easy finding the way on the narrow roads which are
poorly signposted.

We drive through a very small village with a few houses and a tavern. We decide to make a stop and ask about the place.
It feels like going back a hundred years in time. There are some men seated in the shadow of the tavern, having a drink of something.
A goat is walking around inside the tavern and one of the walls have pictures and old bills from all around the world

We sit down in the shadow and a man comes to take our order of something cold to drink.
We ask the owner of the tavern and he tells us how to get to the place we are looking for. Eventually we leave.
What we don´t know at the time is that we will meet the man called Lucky many more times during the journeys we will do with groups of people for healing work.

And so we drive along the meandering roads further and further up in the mountains. Finally it´s not possible to drive any longer but we are walking the last bit. A weird feeling of both sadness and happiness comes over me as we walk in silence this last stretch to the point of the Throat chakra. It feels as if I´ve been here before in a previous life.

The place is desolate with a fantastic view. Amounts of yellow flowers are growing here, dried due to the season. This is the place we have been looking for and jointly we laugh over having found it. A peace spreads at the depth of my heart.

The technological development of the Earth

Human children, the last 100 years you have developed more and more technical and revolutionary things. One technical thing after another has been developed. Finally you have almost stopped marvelling about it. The same development technology has been going through, you will now go through yourselves. Yes, imagine if you could see yourselves in a hundred years from now. You would be amazed, you might even faint, fall into chock or a coma. We laugh and rejoice from this dimension and follow you and what is happening in eager anticipation.
Have faith and trust, beloved human children. We are with you from this dimension. We love and rejoice with you.

In the coming autumn during one of the trips to Greece we visit the point of the Throat chakra with a group joining us. This place were used to stimulate the force of the Goddess both on-site as well as within ourselves. But it will both purify and strengthen the Throat chakra as well.

It´s an amazing feeling for all of us to visit the location and several of the participants experience contact with previous lives. There is a profound healing triggered inside of us.

During the same journey we had decided to pay a visit to a place of worship called Lizos. But obviously we are not. We are actually physically prevented to make this visit, we were planning to do with our group. My husband's back freezes and I sprain my foot. It can´t be more obvious than that. The message is loud and clear. At the moment we´re not going to Lizos.

Instead we go to the location in the mountains, to Lucky which we visited earlier the same week. After making the decision both Stefan's back and my foot feel better. We meditate and hike and it is a very nice ending to the group trip.

After the end of the course and when the participants have left we set off to the north eastern parts of Crete to find an accommodation adjacent to the point of the Sakral chakra. We´ve decided to visit the location with an upcoming group.

Stefan is interested in everything related to places of worship and he would definitely like to take me and our daughter to the archaeological excavation at Malia. My husband visited the excavation many years ago.
I don´t like to come along as a feeling of heaviness comes over me.
My stubborn dear of a husband is pushing me and finally I tag along. When we get there we understand why there was a heavy feel to it. The location is an ongoing excavation site and amounts of souls have for various reasons decided to remain at the scene.

Visual pictures from past lives are being played in my mind and I see myself as a mistreated slave, beaten, raped and deprived of my child, whom in this life is our common daughter. I can see my husband as a so called superior on the construction site. I spot my daughter with one of the men who took her from me. Her beautiful appearance gives her the means to cope and survive.

I die a long and agonizing death from a stab in the genital area, by the man who took my daughter from me. The poor, wretched woman, me in this life, no wonder I wanted to avoid going to this site. But as we know there´s a reason for everything.

We assist all the souls on the excavation site Malia, wanting help to cross over to the light on the other side and a feel of relief arises as we drive away from the excavation site. Following day we go back home to Sweden.

Same summer I´m visited by Merlin during my meditations in our circle of stones. He appears in every meditation and calls on me time after another to make a trip with my husband to Glastonbury in England.

At first I whisk it away and dismiss it but Merlin stubbornly continues to call on me. Merlin is not a helper I´ve been in contact with before. But I know him from the world of fairy tales.
Every time we meditate in the circle of stones he´s standing there awaiting me. During the meditation I argue with him there is no money to make the journey. It results in him visually dragging me to the store and workshop on the farm, where he point out things we can sell to raise the money.

I tell my husband all about it and we put out adverts of the objects we can sell. And we raise a decent amount of money.

In the midst of the summer we go to England and stay in Glastonbury. Using Glastonbury as a base we then visit different power places like crop circles and Stonehenge.

My husband and I come to the understanding during the journey, that we are going to make more trips and we will bring other people to spread the experience of the crop circles and Glastonbury. It´s a very unique power place.

Glastonbury is also said to be the Heart chakra of the world or has a connection to it. Many myths and legends tell of Glastonbury.

Glastonbury, this fascinating place has been a place of worship for thousands of years and was already in the time of Atlantis a place of big importance. Even today we can feel the energies from different Ley lines which were laid out during that time several thousands of years ago.
Today these are known as the Michael-line, the Maria-line and the Maria Magdalena –line.

The Ley lines are extra tangible on the Tor. The Tor is a place, to where the monks in the olden days went on the labyrinth path, up the hill called the Tor. According to the legend, there is a big dragon lying beneath the Tor. Even today the energies are significantly tangible and a magical feel arises at the bear sight of this place.
You can almost feel the druids and the monks walk towards the top. If you sit under the light of the full moon up here, time stands still and it´s simply magic.

Bride´s Mound is located here as well and is known as the entrance to Avalon. Avalon is where priestesses, magicians and druids existed. Only the initiates could find their way through the mists which were said to be surrounding the island. This is one of the places in Glastonbury affecting me the strongest.
It gives me a feeling of recognition and it feels like coming home. Another place with strong energies is Chalice Wells. This site is also a Holy garden and water from the Holy Spring runs

through here. According to the legend it´s believed this is where the Holy Grail is buried.

Water

In the fifth dimension water is a divine beverage which value you have realized. Chemicals, poison and other substances poisoning the water are forbidden. To cleans and charge the water with energies needed for every occasion is as common as using the coffee maker today. Water is treated with care and with the insight that coming generations of human children, animals, and nature are completely dependent on its powers for their continuous development and existence. Therefore you now worship the water like a Goddess with the life-giving power.

There is a very clear message we should manufacture drops of water for the use on the seven different chakras, by using water from the spring on different locations in this magnificent garden. And we do.
Yes, to visit this fantastic place really is a memory for life. The feeling of belonging here gives us a strong longing to come back again.

We return home after some tumultuous days in Glastonbury visiting Stonehenge, Crop circles, The Tor, Bride's Mound, Chalice Wells and much more.
We just have to go there again, and we wouldn't go alone.
The sensation of taking other people to this fantastic place was so strong and it was already decided.

Energies

You are all linked together through different forms of energy and with the help of meditation and contemplation you have the ability to reconnect to the origin of your true self.

Many of you are and will be reconnecting to the contact of your origin. The pure source of energy is now available and many people are now reconnecting to the energies you refer to as Arch Angels as well as Christ, Maria, Maria Magdalena. Those energies carry vibrations making you more coherent with the code of your soul and your origin.
With the help of a visual image you might find it easier to connect, or simply by using the feel link your energies to their energies.
You all work in different ways, consciously or unconsciously, under the influence of certain energies and with the guidance from your higher self, you may find places and situations helping you to find the way home to your own energy.
Human children you already know of this within yourselves. Layers and layers of darkness will be peeled off from you to allow these energies to emerge.

One day I'm contacted by a woman to make a so called spirit scanning and space clearing at her and her husband's home. I've done such many times before but unlike any other time, I get the feeling I'm being stopped on my way to see the woman. I encounter two different car superintendents on my way to see the woman and in the corner of my eye I see a man, it looks like he's wearing a priest's upholstery. I realize someone is trying to prevent this meeting from happening for a reason I'm not aware of.

76

The woman I´m seeing has for a long time been bothered by a headache. She also tells me she´s felt imprisoned in her own home for a very long time.

During the clearing of spirits in the house the man wearing the priest upholstery reappears. We learn he had a very negative view of women. He is helped to cross over to other side. Or anyway, that is what I believe.

A little time passes after the contact with the woman and she lets me know their home is calmer and her headache is gone. In addition she feels much freer.

Six months later we hold a work shop with the Essences of Inner Peace. Following we´re having a course called energy thieves. It is to learn about spirits of trauma and trauma circles.

Two women sign up for the course of energy thieves.
As these two women sign up for the course, a few others unregister after already having signed up for it.

This makes us confused. Nevertheless we decide to conduct the course.
Later we realize what is happening under the course is not supposed to be disturbed by to many other people being involved.

With a smaller group of women we start the course. Throughout the course it appears that one of the women is carrying an old spirit which we understand is a priest from the 1800 century. We get both the name of the priest and during what years he was active. This can be confirmed later on.

On the course we learn the first woman I helped is still carrying that priest with her. He hasn't crossed over to the other side like we thought. We realize we have two different priests needing our help to cross over to the other side. We notice similar patterns in both of these priests.

The pattern of oppression and abuse of power is especially directed towards women and children. This is the link between the priests.

Their presence have in turn affected both of the women carrying them, in a negative way.

Now a prolonged process starts to help the two priests cross over.

The day after the course Stefan has to leave work and go home as he's completely out of energy and feel ill.

He comes home and discovers he caught a so called spirit of trauma from the woman. We call the two women and decide we're coming to their home and through joint forces finally get the priest over to the other side.

At the home of one of the women, my husband finds energy lines running from the church to her house. The same line runs through parts of the other woman's house as well, neighbouring the first house.

We go home and think the mission is finally completed. But alas, we are deceiving ourselves.

The woman's headache picks up and she doesn't feel well so she contacts us again.

We find out the priest has tricked us into believing we helped him to cross over. We understand none of the priests couldn't care less if a woman says anything to them. Hence we

78

understand we need to ask some men for help to make the priests cross over to the other side.

The woman's brother and a good friend of ours come to help us sending the priest to the other side. After a very long time and lots of persuasion the three men is finally successful in helping him over.

We continue to the church to disconnect the line running to the woman's house. This line which has been running straight through her bed in the bedroom, has been the cause of her not being able to sleep in it. But even her dogs have very clearly shown, they don't like lying there.
We understand the priest has been affecting her and making her feel bad in different ways. This seems to be associated to a past life she has lived with this priest. In that life he has also been abusive to her.

We are invited to the women and we are sitting drinking coffee. My husband notices that on the placemats on the table, there is a map with pictures of different churches.
Not a coincidence of course.

As he detects on the place mats, there are straight lines running between the churches, the woman can see a pattern. She has lived on different places within these lines her whole life.
Is it possible she been drawn to those places herself?

Later on we are contacted by the other woman who was in need for help again. They are moving from the farm where the priest has been and problems keep popping up with the buyers of the farm. They are wondering if it might have something to do with the priest.

We go there and as we examine the farm we discover three different energy lines going from the church into their house. These lines must be disrupted to initiate the sale of the farm. We understand this priest is just as awkward and difficult to help cross over to the other side, as the other priest was.

Once again we have to call for some men to help the priest to the other side. We use joint forces. This is the one time I'm actually scared and thinking of interrupting the whole thing. But I gather my courage as I realize it´s just another trick of the priest.

As we help him to the other side, we discover a woman is still there and she is connected to the priest. It appears she´s been taking care of the priest when he was a child, but she has been abusive towards him. This in turn has made him committed to assaults and engaged in abuse of power. She´s also being helped to cross over. After this hundreds of souls from both animals and people appear. It seems now that the priest is gone the other souls dare to come forward.

These poor souls have been threatened and told to believe in hell, to where they are going if they have done something sinful, which most of them have one time or another.

There are many souls granted forgiveness of sins and helped into the light.

This is the start of another major insight, of this being a phenomena having occurred in many churches. And we understand we are being assisted from the other side, in helping these thousands of souls cross over. These souls have been attached at sites, churches and cemeteries in fear of going to hell.

We understand and relate this to the fact, somehow it has to do with the frequency change now happening on earth. We are moving from the fourth to the fifth dimension.

Most old churches have been built on places of worship. Therefore we understand we must clear and move blockages present in those churches and on cemeteries to make it possible to raise the energy to the new frequency.

Blockages

There is an energy grid around mother earth, like a web. It can be compared to man's meridian system, the energy lines you use in acupuncture therapy. As we spoke of earlier everything consists of energy. You human children are a micro cosmos and around you mother earth is a bigger cosmos and the strands of energy you have around your body are correspondingly present around the earth and continues out into cosmos and the universe.

Everything is linked together and the blockages you human children have in your energy system you can also find on your mother earth.

It is important you loosen up blockings in your energy system, but it is also of importance the earth receives help and healing to remove the blockages present on her.

Around what you call churches there are often major blockages, but also around power places. Around the churches there are often major blockages and we see many dead souls gathered and thus blocking a free flow of energy. These are lost, scared and sad souls in need of your help. As you help them cross over the blockages disappear and a free flow will occur.

From the beginning these places are Holy places, from which you human children have received power. It is where you connected to your Goddess and God.

Then as religion and the men of the church seized the power they adopted those places as well, to control them and gain more power, force and energy.

This is a very effective way of stealing the power, the energy from you human children. We can give you more examples of how this has happened and is happening throughout your history.

But returning to the blockages
Your priests and other men of the church also seized the power from women. By oppressing and ridiculing the woman and writing down words about her in an oppressive manner in what you refer to as the Bible, power was taken away from woman and she was turned into a slave and a servant.

Many assaults have been made on both women and children and even today these brutal assaults take place by threats, violence and abuse of power. These forces of darkness.

To steel what means most from a person is a very effective way of seizing the power from her.

To mutilate and ridicule the Holy power of the woman has been effective means.

Consider yourselves what you have been deprived through history.

It is time to restore the balance.

We realize the task of cleaning churches and places with lost souls is far too big for us to carry out alone. So we ask for help from our friends and course attendees with this work. We start a group with the assignment to clear churches from old souls. Through medial messages we learn which churches needs to be cleared and how it shall be done. Every time we are surprised of how many souls there are, needing our help to cross over at each occasion.

Along the way an old friend comes to our home for a visit. She's rather excited and wants to tell us about the new energy grid now being built.
By listening to her we understand the importance of cleaning and clearing the old places to help the new energy grid.

Together we continue clearing churches and help old souls cross over.

Then another piece of the puzzle appears. One of our participants in energy medicine needs help to clear her house.

One Friday night, pretty worn out after a week's work, we visit her and her husband to help them clear their house.
On our way there, I ask my husband for some extra help as tiredness is starting to take its toll on me. We eat a joint meal. After dinner we get up to make the clearing of their house. My husband gets an indication from his divining rod he is not supposed to measure this time, but I shall tune in medially to find out what it's all about.

Immediately comes a message, there is a line passing diagonally through the site and the couple's house and that it's a so called Ley line. This Ley line obviously has its epicentre by the Kivik grave. But it sounds unlikely since it´s located several kilometres away from the couples house.

We ask the couple to produce a map, to find out if this is correct. -Yes, the man in the house says, we have plenty of maps since one of my hobbies is collecting maps.

As a number of maps is on the table, we choose the one containing the most heritage sites. We´re struck by amazement as we see the line between the grave of Kivik and their house is straight as an arrow, and with the fact the line runs straight through the house, just like the information I received medially said.

We notice as well, the line runs straight through the church in the village where they are living. There is also information about how they can protect themselves and what we shall do about the line from the grave of Kivik, which must be cleared as well. We´re tired when leaving the couple and dazed. We have had new staggering insights. Further ahead there will be more.

Places and their energies

Some places on mother earth are ancient sites of worship and for some reason you return time after another. We see how you gather on these sites. Maybe you do not yourselves understand what fore or why you do.
The energy present at these sites possess a specific attraction, it´s almost like a magnetic energy. For example the big pyramids in Egypt which are magical monuments built

thousands of years ago. Maybe you do not understand this with
your conscious mind, but with your higher self this is a place
facilitating contact with us habitants of the Pleiades.
It has been like this for ages. There are many hidden treasures
from the past.
You are now about to find more such places which have been
concealed, hidden and forgotten. They stimulate the contact with
us and awaken the memory of who you are, dear human
children. An amount of places you are about to visit, stimulate
the feminine energy and power of the Goddess. Just like you
know how to stimulate corresponding points on your body
through acupuncture, you can find similar points to stimulate on
mother Earth.
This is why it is also very important to resolve blockages around
your so called churches, as they are ancient sites of the
Goddess, with female energy. Resolving the blockages there will
restore the balance between male and female.
Gather in groups and help the souls being trapped on these
places, to cross over. Thus you help the healing of the earth and
the feminine energies will finally flow freely. Many men of the
churches who through the centuries have oppressed women and
the female energies, will have to give way to the forces of nature
and in amazement and rage be forced to let go.

Time passes and life with courses and educations continues.
After a weekend holding a course I feel much drained of energy
and I ask my husband to measure with his divining rod what
might help.

With the divining rod he finds out we should go to Ale´s stones
after the course to have me cleansed and cleared from heavy

energies. Well at site on Ale´s stones there is information I should lie down on a stone in the centre of the ship.

My husband is standing by one of the stones and experiences he´s been standing there in a previous life. He experience he is not alone but there are people from another time standing at every stone. With the help of drums and vocals they are assisting in what shall take place with the stone and me.

I lie down across the stone with my head towards the ground, and in an instant visually find myself underground. There, I´m met by a beautiful woman telling me I´m in with Hades in the underworld. A small drama unfolds and I´m being tested in my fear of death.

What is old shall die

Death is an occurrence many of you fear and feel anxious about. Many of you feel anxiety at the bear thought of it. Dear children and collaborators, death is merely a symbol of mind but throughout history it has been following you like a wraith. We wish to bring light and awareness that your soul is eternal and invincible
Death in itself is merely a transition from one stage to another. You move through different dimensions. You visit these dimensions at night and this is also where your beloved ones who have "died" exists. We wish to bring light and awareness about death and the presence of death in every breath. In between your breaths a void is formed, which we can call death. By spending time there your soul will be in contact with eternity and the energy of immortality.

Death is a word you human children have learned to
misinterpret as something horrific. There is only a thin veil
between the dimensions. Practice and meditation makes it
possible for you to be in contact with the other side in seconds.
You might not believe this is true, because through the centuries
you have been scared and oppressed by various representative
of religions.
They proclaim you should remain strictly within limits.
If you do not behave like they have determined, you may be
punished and even end up in hell. We must laugh at this
madness and we see what man has created with oppression,
power, control and fear. We are close to you and in times like
these, as the distance between the world's decreases, you can
almost physically experience this.

After this I'm admitted to Hades in the underworld and he
shows me a ship we will travel in.

My husband shall stand in the back to steer and I shall stand in
the front to feel the energy and to send light and healing. This
ship is a symbol of the ship formation of stones, Ale's stones.

Suddenly there is a visual image. There is a herd of Polar bears
in front of me. One of them speaks to me. It says:
-We need help from you people because the ice is melting away
quickly here. The energy grid above earth needs repairing and
building to establish the balance. Help us with the line from
where you are now and send a visual line of light across the
ocean. And then receive the line of light from the opposite side.

A strong sense of light comes over me. The images disappear
and I notice how uncomfortable it is to be lying on the cold and

hard stone. Dazed I get up, my husband and I look at each other, laughing. We notice the visitors around us are looking at us wondering what we are actually doing. Well, we are wondering ourselves as well, but somehow it all feels absolutely right and good.

Filled with the event we go home and decide to once again ask for help from friends and course participants.

We are going to help the Polar bears and send energy of light and power from the bow of the ship in Ale´s stones, out over the sea and across the earth and back again to the other side of the ship. There is information, there should be a man and a woman standing by every other stone all the way round. This gives us a bit of a headache, since it´s mostly women assisting us during these occasions.

We decide to entrust it to higher powers and start sending e-mails to our friends and course participant's a few days prior to the aid effort.

Early in the morning of the event, I´m awakened by someone from the other side giving me the information a network will be formed associated to the aid effort from Ale´s stones.

This will be the beginning of Friends of Mother earth, a network to support, develop and raise awareness of the energy increase from the fourth to the fifth dimension.

𝕸other earth´s cry for help

For a long time, mother earth has cried out for you and from our dimension we see how shut down and cut off you are from yourselves and mother earth. Darkness has ruled for thousands of years and the imbalance between male and female energy has caused this. To hear her call for help and to open up yourselves, you shall let light, love and peace within.

In various ways we have given you perspectives of this and we now believe you understand the importance of restoring the balance so that at last, the healing love energy may be released upon earth. The new time that has come, can finally be manifested. Only what you in the depth of your heart and soul long for and dream about on earth is

Peace, Love, Harmony, Joy and Happiness.

Ale´s stones 10-10-2010

This particular Sunday when we were doing the reinforcement of energy, happened to be on the date of 10-10-2010. We are aware many likeminded, working with healing and energy work around the world, are doing it simultaneously with our aid effort. Naturally this gives us extra energy and power.

Both my husband and I are happy and surprised when we come to Ale´s stones and discover almost every stone has a man and a woman standing next to it and that the amount of men is almost as many as women.

The last help from the other side appears as light essences who placed themselves by the empty stones to assist. The ship's crew has become fully stretched.

Our mission to help our mother earth and the polar bears feels successful.

The summer of 2010 I have a summer course with participants training for Energy medicine.

One of the days during the course we visit the Heimdall stones and we spend a wonderful day in nature. As we arrive at the site, a lot of raven and crows are circuiting above the place. We understand it is a message from the other side and during the day the energies cry out. I feel a strong impulse I should channel a message to the group. We make a ring sitting down on the stones and following message comes.

It does not feel easy

It is such a long time since I was in a body. It might be easy for you, walking in it all the time, but to us from other dimensions it is heavy. We wish to be here to help you. We see all that you do, what you are in the midst of, what you fight for in your lives. Dear children, we are with you from the other side. You are never alone, you might think so, but you never are. In different ways we try to convey ourselves to you, but you are so preoccupied (laughter), or so you think (laughter). But really, you already know that preoccupation is about something completely different. What are you running after? Do you know yourselves? Probably not, it looks so funny (laughter) from our point of view (laughter).

Do you realize when you are running towards a personal goal or when you are not? You run towards your own death. What you refer to as death is really a transition to our side. We understand you are in a hurry to come home to us. But my dear children, you have an assignment and that is why you are here. To find that assignment you need to look within. You cannot find it around you. Around you it is a myriad like that of an ant hill. Have you also seen an anthill above ground? But are you aware underground there is a similar one, just reversed? It is the same with you, what is visible to your eyes is just a part of you. But like the anthill, you carry just as much within not visible to the eye. It is where the most important of all is happening. Your assignment is to see and find out what is there.

You are the children of the light, therefore it might be extra heavy to you. There is a darkness on the earth at the moment. Find your way to each other, find your way out from the darkness, and find your way towards the light! But the light has a different appearance to each one of you. The beauty of life is the light, what feels good for you is the light. Sometimes the light becomes bright just like this sunny day. Sunbathe with moderation, the light must grow at its own pace. What feels right to one person, feels wrong to the other. The answer you carry within.

We need to speed up development on earth. It is up to all of you. From another dimension it looks simple but we know it can be difficult for you standing in the middle of it. Find out where you

are in your development. Obstacles must be removed. One
obstacle is fear. It is a feeling familiar to all of you.
It is like a blocked drain. The blockage has to go, be removed to
once again allow a free flow.
Once you have removed the obstacle you will get new energy to
proceed forward on your path without barriers, the path leads
you forward. Sometimes you shall walk around the various
obstacles to remove the fear. The light and the darkness is in a
respective pan balance. Make your own choice where to put
your strength. Think, before you make your choices. Dear
children, we are with you. Learn how to ask for your wishes,
from us. The earth is a part of yourselves, even you can feel the
earth is shaking.
Ask for help, cry out and call!
Do not walk alone!
Listen to the answer you receive during meditations!
Walk in silence!
We are with you!
We will be seeing you again.

An "Orb" on a photo from the night after our message channelling at Heimdall´s stones, during the summer course in energy medicine 2010. (Photo Christian Svensson).

After a lovely day we go home and during the night we have a very pleasant get-together. We have a bite and socialize. This is when some photographs are taken by one of the students. What is seen on many of the photographs are several round circles. Those circles are called orbs and they are energies from spirits. Just like after the message during the day, we know we are not alone.

onnectedness

To be associated to someone or to be in the larger context of a group is something we wish to encourage. Through these meetings new forms of life and magic arises.
In the conversations you have new ideas will form and concrete solutions emerge to problems which sometimes sit like blockages in your lives.

It is now important for you to seek out groups or people being open and free in thought and feeling.
Do not be judgemental towards each other, be open and attentive to yourselves, your feelings and reactions. Let them be a reflection showing who you are, where you are in your progress.
Many of the people you meet on your life's journey are soul's reflecting what you yourself should be attentive to.
First you need to pay attention, stop and reflect on what role you have in your life's drama. And as you see what these meetings with other people wish to tell you, you can say thanks, let go and move on to the next meeting.

The summer of 2010 I´m woken up in the middle of the night and I´m urged from the spirit world to meditate and do a five days retreat. During these five days I will be alone with myself and get guidance about what is to come. It´s also important I´m in nature at the time.

By now I have learned to put a lot of faith in the messages and directions I receive from the spirit world and I realize they are important.

Go out into nature

Reconnect to nature. Nature carries all the answers. Everything is linked in a symphony of colours, shapes and materials.
Feel the trunk of the tree, see the colour and the shape of the flower and the greenery's vibration of life giving energy and healing power.

Fill your breaths and your mind with oxygen and let it move on throughout your entire body and soul. Become one with nature and you will understand how everything is intertwined.
Everything is linked together for all eternity. Study the animals and see their unique abilities. Learn from them and integrate that in your being, you beloved human children.
Then you will understand the grandness and how vibrating and life giving nature is.
Take the step back into nature where you belong.

I do the retreat and there are many thoughts appearing to me during this time. One question that keeps coming back in mind, is how to best protect us from negative energies wanting to affect us and counter us in our ongoing light work. I'm instructed to use certain selected crop circles. They are to be protective but in addition we shall use stones in different colours. These stones are placed in a triangle. The triangle is found as a connection to different places on earth. I don't know what this means at the time. When later I get three words to go with the triangle I put them down in writing. After this they fall into oblivion. And I return to everyday life.

Protect yourselves and your crystal

In times like these it is important to protect yourselves and your crystal. Now darkness and light will meet and then new energies appear. You can compare it to thunder when warm and cold air meet, but now the meeting is between darkness and light.
We have told you earlier of what energies darkness is connected to but also which ones the light is connected to.
From our dimension we see an ongoing war between those two forces. Therefore it is of utmost importance you are particularly careful about what people and energies you surround yourselves with. Many souls and human children are so filled of darkness, they want to counter light and the people chosen to move from the fourth to the fifth dimension, in every way possible. The light dazzles in the dark and to darkness there is a bigger gain holding on to darkness than letting the light in. The light is reminding the darkness of all the pain that has been buried and hidden underneath for a very long time.
That is why light is a choice you make dear human children. But you shall also become and be more aware of the major benefit you gain, by choosing the light. It is love, peace and light and an earth with more balance making it possible for you to become the radiant souls you are. Within, the war is ongoing and the

struggle between darkness and light is constantly present.
Meditation is a powerful tool to raise awareness and remove
darkness, so that you can finally let go of that ancient, heavy
coat darkness has been to you.
Seek for groups of people, to find the support for your inner
journey of peace.
Let meditation be part of your everyday life and in your life.

Time passes and the telepathic messages comes more and more
frequent. An intense period of writing starts. My husband and
our children find me sitting by the kitchen table at all sorts of
weird times during the day. Usually I´m awoken at night to be
able to write undisturbed.

I´ve always enjoyed writing and drawing, but I´m aware what
I´m writing at the moment is something completely different.
Soon enough a certainty arises it´s actually a book I´m writing.

What finally makes me realize this fact, is when I during a
séance receive a message for a woman she will start to write. At
the same time a wonderful angel essence is appearing, handing
over a pen to her but one to me as well. For me, she has a very
thick book and tells me to write. And then she says:
-It has already been written.
The message feels very powerful and I cannot get it out of my
mind.

The book is coming more and more together and the telepathic
messages are more frequent. There is a vision showing a picture
of a funnel. We will pass through it going from the fourth to the
fifth dimension. Like a lightning from the clear blue I see the
message of the same triangle as I did during the retreat. But now

there are two triangles, meeting point to point. These points slowly start moving towards each other, forming the funnel we´re going through. The two triangles are now united, forming a six-pointed star. In the middle of the star an eye is emerging. Eventually more fragments of images from places are appearing. Along with them different colours can be seen in the points. They turn out to be the same as the colours of the chakras.

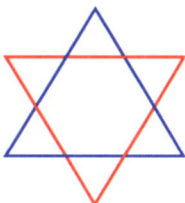

Afterwards the staggering insight comes to mind, this is an instruction from the Pleiades of points to be stimulated. They are to be used in helping earth and its people in the transition from the fourth to the fifth dimension.

The points and places emerging are:

1. Egypt is red. It´s linked to the pyramids.

2. England is green. It´s linked to Glastonbury and the crop circles.

3. France is purple and linked to the grave of Maria Magdalena.

4. Spain is orange and has a link to El Camino.

5. Italy is yellow with a connection to the headscarf of Christ and Damanhur which is a power place.

6. Finally Greece which is blue and linked to an old site of the Goddess.

These tips of the star are found as junctions around the Globe and from the stars in heaven threads are reaching out, now forming the new grid of energy.
There is an eye in the middle of the star, "the Third eye".
As some of you know the Third eye, which can be seen on the one dollar bill and on the emblem of the Freemasons, is only meant for the initiates of the mystery of inner seeing. This eye symbolizes the ability of seeing into obscurity. As you see the completed star, the eye will fall into place in the middle.

When these triangles merge to form the star, "seeing" now becomes possible to all humans who wants to, as we move from the fourth to the fifth dimension. The Eye will fall into place in the chest and Heart chakra. Here the circle comes to a close. Everything old dies allowing the new to be born. The new time in the fifth dimension.

This transition is one of the causes, events we see around us today are much more powerful and stronger than they have been for a very long time.
This also implies, we here on earth have a major opportunity to influence the universal change in a very positive way. We can choose a process of peace and make our own inner journey. We can choose to live in peace with ourselves and other people.

Earth, just like people, consists of both Yin and Yang. Thus both female and male energy. The star points belonging to Europe are connected to both Yin and Yang. But there are similar points all around the world. The points in Europe seem to have means for activating.

In Chinese medicine the fire element has a strong transformational impact on various processes of the body. If we transfer this to earth, we can through activating corresponding points help the earth and the universe in the transformation to the fifth dimension.

There seems to be six different stars being activated right now, in the new energy grid. The seventh star is mother earth herself. That makes three stars on one half of the earth and three on the other. Out of the three, one is female and one male and one is both female and male in its energy. Together those six stars form a grid assisting in holding up the fifth dimension.

All of these stars are interconnected to one another. Energy lines running from their points form a grid. This grid continues further out in the universe with threads of energy running through the various dimensions.
This might be the reason we are able to use the power places such as the pyramids in Egypt, to facilitate reconnection with the Pleiades and other dimensions through time and space. Therefore to meditate on the sites of these power points is a very strong experience.

This tapestry of energy and light is the future means of transportation. It´s all in the tapestry. Through it we can reconnect with other dimensions. We can see the occurrence of all meetings and all the events unfolding.

During late autumn I start the continuance of my education in Denmark. It is now I will come to the insight it´s a "mission" to spread the message of Peace from the Pleiades. It is of utmost importance.

There are forceful messages of this in meditations and I know there is more information to come of how it will proceed. But for now I will have to bide my time.

Everything moves faster now

We spoke to you of time and how at the moment it is moving faster. It might be difficult to understand as your system consists of obsolete principles of what time really is. Time is eternal but does not exist the same way at all here with us, as it does with you on earth.
To us habitants of the Pleiades, time is energy and infinitely present. To you it is a limitation and a guideline, belonging to the fourth dimension's way of thinking and acting. To us in the tenth dimension, it means energy moving us forwards or backwards, sideways, upwards or downwards. Yes, any direction we like to travel. This way we use time and light as means of transportation. To you it might seem odd and crazy. To us it is a fact. There are many among you on earth, feeling a change in time which you cannot grasp. Trust your feel, it will lead you right.

The messages from the Pleiades continue to come.
In addition it contains messages and suggestions of different methods people can use during the journey of peace.
This raises many thoughts and like a little ball of snow, they soon grow into a giant ball of ideas for the continuing work.

Eventually a therapy forms out of all this, which will help us make a journey to create peace with ourselves and our earth. The Inner Peace Journey.

Inner Peace Journey

Making your Inner Peace journey is a conscious choice, involving work with your inner self. By feeling at peace with ourselves and within, peace is created in the outer. You can look upon it as a reflection of one another, i.e. the outer reflects the inner and the inner reflects the outer. This work with ourselves can commence now and is a conscious choice we can make for ourselves, each other and the earth.

It is our own responsibility as a Citizen of the World.

Your decision to make the Inner Peace Journey affects the grid and all the people around us is affected. Your light and energy increases as you peel off your masks. This light continues to vibrate further out in the grid.

In the time we are now living, we go through some kind of elevation of awareness and a transformation from the fourth to the fifth dimension.

If you like you can convert this to an image of man with the seven chakra points. From having found ourselves at the Solar plexus chakra we now move towards the Heart chakra.
If we take a closer look at the chakra points, the energy of the Solar Plexus chakra is imbalanced, as for example "I" is a pretty egocentric way of thinking – war, control and power.

This means the male energy, which have been dominating on earth for a long time, must decrease and leave a bigger space for the female energy thus bringing more balance and harmony to our earth.
And if we take a look at the world, the male energy has been in the superiority for a very long time. What we are now moving towards is the heart being the female, positive energy linked to love, empathy, happiness, beauty and peace.

This is not about man or woman but about our values. What is of importance? Which are the values we allow to control our lives? A lot of what we see around the world is connected to the male energy.

So we are in the end of one cycle and the beginning of a new. It can feel chaotic, being in this space between old and new. Everything we used to think was important might all of a sudden seem unimportant and we choose new values as focal points in our lives.
This is just as it should be.
To comply with that change and to adjust makes it less painful and difficult, gaining access to the new.

Many thousands of years ago an electromagnetic field was created around earth. This grid was connected to the universe to provide man with energy and information from cosmos.
For the first time in 10 000 years earth has now reached a frequency making it possible to create a new electromagnetic field to help reaching the fifth dimension.

The new grid is located about a meter above the earth's surface and Holy places are created for these energy fields.

They create openings and make interdimensional journeys possible. It also creates communication with ethereal essences. The energy field is used for sending messages between the spirit world and us. It helps us understand our spiritual assignment and life's mission.

It helps us sending love and healing to each other. It also helps the initiates to open the third eye on their way towards enlightenment. It unites the world into one.
It increases the ability of manifesting our wishes both for ourselves and for others. The earth's magnetic field is strengthened into the light and connects humanity with mother earth.

People around you may react in different ways when you make your inner peace journey. Some might encourage you. Others get angry and scared and distances themselves from you. Some might want you back in your old roll and others might even scold at you. Yes, there will be many different reactions when the light from you vibrates stronger out in the grid. Therefore it´s important for you to stay balanced and focused. With the help of meditation it will be easier.

The war within you

The war now going on within you, is a result of thousands of year's oppression of your own being's true self. A battle between darkness and light which has been going on for eons of time.

It is a struggle of power for good or bad, and an unwillingness to let go of the old self's pain and mask you have all been carrying since the beginning of time. Now the time has come to leave the trodden path and the old footprints to explore many new astonishing dimensions and occurrences. You are standing right on the threshold of a new presence, a new life on your earth.

Through meditation and by staying in contact with your inner self you are helped in the transition to the fifth dimension. Through "the journey" you are also trained in the universal school in different things such as

trust, patience, courage and love for yourselves. It includes setting boundaries and daring to let go of the old.

We encounter different *resistance*s during the journey and it's important to know, because those resistances can hold deep fear of change and of going through change. Our *ego* wants us to stay in our old familiar patterns.
We all have different life patterns and those patterns are present until we see and understand what we shall learn from them and what we have to let go off. Making journeys back to previous lives can help us to let go of old fears and limitations.

Perhaps we can see the read thread running through our lives and now back to previous lives as patterns of for example fear, guilt, and sorrow.
This pattern and blockages can be found in the fourth dimension's grid.

Almost like a fisherman, removing debris from his fishing net, you remove your blockages but on an emotional and mental level. Using the onion as a symbol, we peel off layer after layer to reach all the way to our inner core, our crystal.

We can therefore look upon these blockages as darkness to be dispelled. The darkness can be fears, sorrow, control, anger, hatred, oppression within us. The darkness around us may consist of war, drugs, medicines, poisons and other addictive's

Old values will die

The values you human children have built as walls will now be demolished. Old fossilised beliefs, ideas of what is right or wrong, good or evil, good or bad shall be changed. Mountains of laws and regulations will be demolished.
From this dimension we see, many of you light souls have already begun this work. We know it is a very hard work both physically and mentally. These core values can be likened to the foundation of a house and may have been good in the fourth dimension but now it starts to wither. Nature and ravages of time is the energy slowly breaking down what you once built up. The building was square, logical and male in its energy and design. Now is the time to build a new foundation where more balanced core values can be like a blessing to human kind and the earth. Feed yourselves with nutrition, light, and love so that you will have the power and energy to build the new.

The light in the darkness

We now speak of the light in the darkness that everyone is looking for on the path towards peace with themselves. Light keeps the flame within you burning and brings courage and strength to believe in the good despite the dark forces around. Light shows the way forward and brings joy in the darkness and helps you to see what is hidden. Light lives in each and every one and it is your own responsibility to keep the flame alive and to spread the light.

As you do this for yourselves you are doing it for your children, relatives, friends, and the earth, yes really across the whole universe. This is one of your most important tasks, to keep the flame alive, but also within. You are a child of light, and now you are peeling off the armour you have been carrying for millions of years. The more space light is given within you, the more light comes to the planet. Everyone can contribute to this. The flame within can be kept alive by listening inwards to the guidance you receive, by listening to your heart, by letting passion be part of your life. You need to work WITH yourselves and not AGAINST yourselves. This means to be honest and true to yourselves. To be your own knight of love, peace and light.

There are various tools such as meditation and healing to begin the peace journey. It affects the increase of consciousness among ourselves and for the earth going from the fourth to the fifth dimension. We can use various symbols. Symbols have been around since time immemorial. Symbols are the language of the universe. It doesn´t matter which language we speak because the language of symbols extends across borders.

The triangle is such a symbol, pointing upwards and downwards.

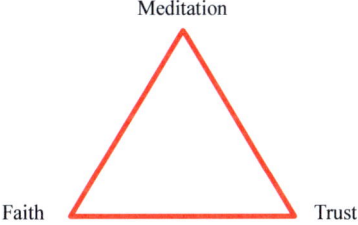

The triangle down from earth, with the point up to the universe for meditation, faith, and the trust in yourselves.

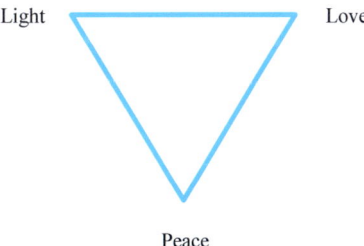

Triangle up from the universe with the point pointing down towards carth for peace, light and love.

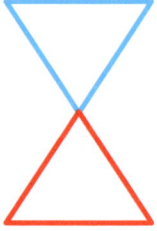

As the tips meet, a funnel forms which symbolically shows rebirth into the fifth dimension. As the tips falls completely in place the six-pointed star emerges and the all Seeing Eye can be seen in the middle.

This shows the third eye has been given a new place in the Heart chakra, and that everyone listening to their heart and making their choices from the heart have the ability to "see" with their inner eye, for them to make good choices both for themselves and the earth.

When the triangles meat and move towards each other a six pointed star is created and the eye will open in the centre. It´s a symbolic image of the Heart chakra and of it being opened. Symbolically the eye is also placed on the chest and Heart chakra and shows the transformation from the fourth to the fifth dimension.

The inner eye and the heart is also connected to the heart of the earth and the universe. The different words in the points of the triangles, carries frequencies that will raise our energy and our consciousness.

Peace: peaceful thoughts and feelings with ourselves, other people, the animals, the earth and the universe.

Love: Loving thoughts and feelings for ourselves, other people, the animals, the earth and the universe.

Light: Light can raise awareness of what is and has been hidden. We can see behind the mask and the words, what darkness is, such as fear, control, power, and oppression. Light is love, joy, peace, gratitude, passion, awareness, clean water and energetic food.

*Meditation: m*akes us more aware and helps us to be more in the present. Darkness is transformed by light to greater awareness. *Meditation and awareness* gives us a contact inwards with our internal. It helps us letting go of the old and gives us a sense of peace.

Trust: Makes it easier to let go of control, pain and negative mind-sets. We can practice daily to gain trust.

Faith: gives us the courage to choose peace.

Believe you can create whatever you want on earth

In times like these with the revolutionary change of dimension, it is of utmost importance together you focus on what is positive and brings joy and love. What you dream of is very close to you now. It is entirely your own choices. Therefore it is very important for you to see what darkness is, and what is light. To find your way in the dark you can use meditation, contemplation, reflection and soul-searching.

Get together in groups and seek the leaders of the new age. The leaders of the new age can help you on your way gaining insights about yourselves, and in receiving help and guidance on how to access your own true self. You shall liberate yourselves from these ages of darkness you have been living with for thousands of years. The leaders of the new age listen to the feel and intuition and make decisions beneficial to the earth and you human children. They make more long term decisions which are not affected by money.

The leaders of the new age know there is an abundance sufficient for everyone. Money are redistributed and will not have the same power over you people. In the new time, the fifth dimension, fundamental values are love, peace, harmony and happiness. It is now at the top of your list. Focus on what is positive and see the negative as darkness to be eliminated. Every human being, we repeat every human being makes his own choice for how the future will be.

For a long time you have believed and been duped to believe, a higher power is in control and that you cannot yourselves affect your future. You believe politicians sit on power. This exists only as long as you accept and believe in it. Never throughout your history, have you had such an opportunity of influencing the transition to the new time, as right now. Do not believe in the doomsday prophesies of Earth's destruction. When you believe

it, you will also create it. We see you divide into different camps.
The ones who believe in prophesies of doomsday - you create it.
The ones who do not think there is any point in doing anything -
you create it.
But you pillars of light, increasing over the earth and believing
in an earth of love, peace and happiness - you create it! Thus
the three different parties are the Earth's Destruction Party,
the Resignation Party and the Love, Light and Peace party.
If you can see this breakdown you may see and understand how
crazy it looks from this dimension where we reside. To us there
is no doubt on which party you should put your vote and join.
See your own darkness, admit and scrutinize yourselves.
Then you can join the party of love peace and light on earth.
The line between darkness and light is subtle and only with your
heart and your inner voice, you will understand the difference.
Search within! Meditation, meditation, meditation.
You need to practice this again and again. We wish to help you,
but this work you can only do yourselves.

The eye inside the star helps us see and hear our inner voice, the
voice of our heart.

Time of enlightenment has come

Meditation can give you light from above and bring insight and perspective to the life you live on your planet. It gives you the insight of what is important to continue working with and what is of importance to let go. The way you are living today, there is a major imbalance between male and female energy. This imbalance is your own creation. When you can see how it has arisen, it will be possible for you to create the balance so many of you are longing for.

Therefore, information and awareness is a very important step towards developing a more balanced earth. Within every human child lies the answer of how a balance can be achieved. You all carry a male and female side, and in order to achieve balance and harmony, both of these sides must be used equally. In yourselves as well as on earth. Today you earthlings are mostly using the so called male component, creating a major imbalance for both the male and female energy in yourselves.

If you can recognize yourselves as a micro cosmos or a reflection of everything around, you will also see what to do with yourselves and the earth to restore the balance.

Transformation

The whole existence you are now living in, is undergoing a major transformation. Time runs faster. What you thought you had time for, a few years ago is now difficult to keep up with. In eras like these it is important to sort out what no longer has a function. What steels power and energy and simply is not your mission shall be removed. Focus your energy on things of real importance to you. Your time and your being is very important.

Imagine you would die in a year. Then decide what is really
important to you in life. Meditate and contemplate on this. It is
like doing a big clean up inside yourselves and your life.
Now, there is no space for irrelevant junk. It is only stealing
your time and energy.

New visions

The new time and new values will now be built with different
building blocks. Thus, getting a common vision is very
important for you human children. Through meditation,
contemplation, retreat and silence you can now find the vision
of how paradise is to be built and created by you human
children. Make clear and distinct images of your common
vision, take help from your new leaders for guidance in the
transition from the old to the new.
Hold on with tenderness and do not force the new, but follow the
natural flow encoded in yourselves and your nature.

Food

We now wish to speak to you about food, and what you drink.
Your entire light body is filled with what you eat and drink. It is
therefore of the utmost importance to ingest food and drink
which is as clean as possible. We would like to give you a
parable. Imagine a candle! If you put in other ingredients in the
candle, it will burn with a poorer flame and perhaps in some

*cases not at all. Similarly it is with your body, the purer food
and beverage the better energy and light you can radiate.
We wish to encourage raw, unprocessed food and beverage
without chemicals. We would like you to SHINE, as you are
meant to, dear human child. Love and honour your bodies and
make conscious choices of food and beverage for your health.
The food available in the fifth dimension is free from additives
and substances that might damage your body. Food is clean and
provide energy and force to carry you, and give energy
vibrating in the frequency you need to fulfil your life's mission.
Food can be seen as a part of the body, and you are what you
eat. Your channel and light body vibrates and enter the
frequency consistent with your inner purpose. In the new
dimension, it is not that common to be ill. To eat meat becomes
less important, but to eat fruits and greens vibrating with more
energy feels more appealing.
To grow organically and to be more self-sufficient becomes
more important. Food tastes of what it is supposed to, without
additives.
In the fifth dimension water is a divine beverage of which you
have understood the value. Chemicals and other substances
poisoning the water is prohibited. To clean and charge the
water with energies needed for the moment is just as common as
making coffee in coffee makers today.
Water is treated with care and with the awareness that future
generations of human children, animals and nature is
completely dependent on its power for their continued existence
and development.
You now worship the water as a Goddess with the life giving
power. Water is in its origin the purest energy. It can also
change form and shape infinitely. You see it on your earth as
rivers, lakes and seas but also as rain, fog, snow and hail.
Through the magic of nature and when the different elements*

come together the water changes its form. Out of the water new life arises. Water is the vivifying principle providing nutrition and support for everything that grows.

Water is the great mother and is the messenger and sign of the Goddess. You can recognize her in all this wonderful life giving water.

We activate our journey of peace with meditation and healing, beautiful colours, music and loving actions. Inner Peace Essences can be helpful, as well as finding the passion in your life. To spend time in nature, to listen inward and to pray will also promote the peace journey.

Eat food vibrating with a higher frequency - fruit, berries, vegetables, lentils, beans, seeds, nuts, vitamins, minerals and herbs, preferably organic and as toxin free as possible. Drink clean water, use images of crop circles, the six pointed star, the triangle, flowers, plants, animals and nature to charge the water with positive energy.

Return of the Goddess

The time has now come for the receiving and female energies to return to your earth. In the fifth dimension there is no longer room for war, power, control, anger and fear. The time of Peace has come and it is you human children, who by using your own power will introduce the new age. Through your internal work which we spoke to you of, you help not only yourself but also those around you, near and dear ones and mother earth.

This is precisely how the energies we spoke of earlier works.
Meditation increases the speed of development. It is just the
same with your own work, each and every one of you can do.
This will help you reaching the fifth dimension of peace,
freedom, love and awareness. There is no external force doing
this for you. Together you form fantastic islands and countries
of light. We follow you with joy and encouragement.

Then comes the last lines of peace messages from the Pleiades

*T*he new age has come and it slowly descends over the earth.
Layers and layers of old energy is now being peeled off, from
you human children as well as from your mother earth. It is as if
all of you as a whole, shedding a giant skin. Everything old dies,
to let the beautiful newly born come forward. We follow you
with excitement, and wish, just for a second you could see what
we see.
From our perspective there is no doubt, no fear or struggle.
We see how you move towards the new time
for peace, light and love.
We will meet again you beautiful human children
with greetings from the Pleiades

Glossary:
Ley lines are energy lines running across the earth.
The lines usually run through places of worship.

Chakra is an energy wheel i.e. whirls of energy on specific parts
of the body.
Chakras are connected to different glands and organs.
They are also associated with colours and different levels of
development in a man's life.

Orbs are energy balls of light, which we quite often see on
photographs today, when using a digital camera.
Orbs are said to be energies of spirits.

Yin and Yang is in Chinese medicine a declaration on the two
energies we have both within us and around us. Yin stands for
the receiving, female principle and Yang stands for the
expansive, male one. These two forces are completely
dependent on each other and cannot exist without the other.
There should be a balance between these two forces for us to
feel well.